ONE WORLD

ONE WORLD

BY WENDELL L. WILLKIE

WITH AN INTRODUCTION BY DONALD BRUCE JOHNSON

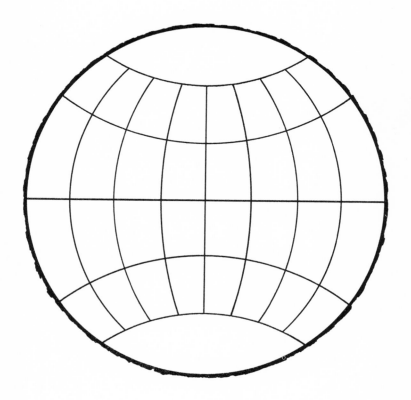

UNIVERSITY OF ILLINOIS PRESS, URBANA AND LONDON, 1966

INTRODUCTION

By Donald Bruce Johnson

WHEN *One World* was published in 1943, it became an immediate best-seller, and to many Americans it was a summary of their aspirations for a free and cooperative world· after the war. The book was written a year and a half after the bombing of Pearl Harbor and fourteen months before the invasion of Normandy, and at the time several problems were on the horizon. The principal question was how the United States would assist other free nations in the defeat of Germany and Japan. There was also much concern about winning the peace so that another war would not be fought in vain, and much speculation about the preservation of freedom in a postwar world. Given the debacle of the League of Nations after World War I, the role of international cooperation in a postwar world reduced in size by technology and interdependence was discussed across the land.

In this milieu *One World* was eagerly received and read; in one form or another more than two million copies were distributed and more than a hundred daily newspapers printed an abbreviated version of the text. It was described as the most influential book published in America during the war and it certainly was a catalyst of thought for many citizens whose views had been inarticulated prior to this time.

Now a new generation has an opportunity to read about Mr. Willkie's travels and to weigh his observations. Fortunately, this new generation is not without a perspective on the action of the early 'forties. The mass media, particularly television, have reproduced through a form of the historical novel the conflict and daily turmoil of those days. The book is more meaningful in this historical perspective, but the significance of the republication of this volume is that Willkie's messages about liberty, domestic imperialism, and freedom of choice ring as freshly and as necessarily as ever. And the difficulties of implementing these goals are as lucid as they were when *One World* was written.

Wendell Willkie, the author of this little book, was a unique figure on the American political scene. Born in Indiana in 1892, he was a normal, precocious student who was graduated from Elwood High School, Indiana University, and later, after a year of teaching history in Kansas, from the Indiana University Law School, where he won every first prize awarded for scholastic achievement. After practicing law for a short time in 1917, he enlisted in the army, served overseas in a legal capacity, and returned a captain in 1919. He joined the legal department of the Firestone Tire & Rubber Co. in Akron, Ohio. Two years later he accepted a position with a firm of utility lawyers. In 1929 he moved to New York to join the legal representatives of a newly formed public utility giant, the Commonwealth and Southern Corporation, and in four years he was its president. This was during the Great Depression, at a time when the utilities were both feared and discredited, and Wendell Willkie spent the next eight years of his life trying to stimulate the industry, improve sales, and fight the government on the issue of public power.

Willkie earned his industrial and political reputation opposing the development of the Tennessee Valley Authority. He vigorously argued his case for American capitalism before Congress, the courts, and the public. Finally, in 1939, the government purchased various privately owned power companies within the Commonwealth and Southern complex for the TVA. Willkie was credited with protecting the investors, and concomitantly he became known as one of the most articulate leaders of the economic community. In his publications and addresses he broadened his criticisms of the Roosevelt administration, from business regulation to economic philosophy in general. As a result, late in that year — only seven or eight months before the national nominating convention of 1940 — Willkie was occasionally mentioned as a Republican presidential possibility.

The incredible part of this development was that Willkie, from the time he grew up in Indiana until 1938, was a registered Democrat! In 1935 he actually was listed as a member of the Tammany County Committee in the Fifteenth Assembly District in New York City. The thought of a utility tycoon who had been a registered Democrat two years earlier as the G.O.P. presidential nominee was anathema to party professionals, but many Republicans found Willkie an attractive and fresh figure on the political scene, as well as a proven tough competitor with, and critic of, the New Deal.

The story of how this dark horse, virtually unknown outside the business community, became the Republican presidential candidate in 1940 is one of the fantastic episodes in American political history. Through the cooperation of thousands of businessmen, advertising leaders, upper middle-class women, lawyers, and many other organized political veterans as well as unorganized and disorganized amateurs in politics, Willkie was publicized and catapulted to fame. He was pictured as a dynamic free-enterpriser who helped reduce the impact of the depression, as a hard-working, homespun, small-town boy, a friendly Horatio Alger type who was the only person qualified to oppose the popular Franklin Roosevelt in his bid for a third term.

The front-runners for the Republican nomination that year were Thomas E. Dewey, then a young New York district attorney; Senator Robert A. Taft of Ohio, a somewhat isolationist favorite of the conservative wing of the party; and Senator Arthur Vandenberg of Michigan, a possible compromise candidate if the others deadlocked. In January Vandenberg was the favorite; by convention time Dewey had the most first-ballot votes, but Taft supporters claimed their candidate had the most total pledges. In April, six weeks before the convention, less than 15 per cent of the American people even knew who Willkie was; by the middle of June he was the outsider whose professionally engineered bandwagon was the chief threat to the established candidates. It was a case of the attractive newcomer against the traditional party forces, and efforts of long-time Republican congressmen to stop the momentum of the Willkie movement proved futile.

At the nominating convention in Philadelphia, several developments proved crucial to the decision reached by the party. First, thousands of constituents sent messages — possibly as the result of the remarkable publicity buildup — urging their delegates to support the attractive Hoosier. Second, galleries filled with Willkie's supporters chanted "We Want Willkie!" at every pause in the proceedings. Third, Dewey, Taft, and Vandenberg, who may have held a majority of the delegates among them when the convention opened, failed to cooperate to defeat the outsider, and thus a vacuum of leadership in the party became apparent. Finally, Willkie was the beneficiary of excellent floor management and support by an experienced group of politicians. They sold their aggressive, fresh, and articulate crusader to the delegates who desperately wanted a winner. Gradually Willkie surged ahead of the rapidly fading professionals. On the fifth ballot, support for the other candidates collapsed and this former Democrat and corporate leader, who had never held or even run for a public office, was nominated as the Republican candidate for the presidency of the United States!

The campaign that followed in 1940 was one of the more dramatic in our history. Pitched to the American people who were ambivalent about the extent to which the United States should be involved in another war, but staged, nevertheless, shortly after the fall of France, and coupled with the first attempt by an American President to seek a third consecutive term in office, it was bitter and confusing. Willkie proved to be a vigorous but inexperienced campaigner who learned quickly — the hard way. He lost his voice, was unable to coordinate his many amateur supporters with the professional party organizations, wasted much of his effort in nonprofitable areas, and generally was unable to convince the voters that he would be a commander-in-chief on the domestic and foreign fronts superior to the President who had had eight years of experience.

One of the difficulties in the attack by Willkie on Roosevelt was that he agreed, by and large, with the Administration's foreign policy. He supported both increased assistance for Britain and selective service. He also agreed with much of the social reform achieved under the New Deal. Thus he was relegated to criticizing such things as the methods used by the Administration, the lack of efficiency in its operation, the supporters of the President, the oppression of free enterprise, and the bureaucratic trend in the United States. Although he traveled 19,000 miles and gave 550 energetic and exhausting speeches, his policy disagreements with the President seemed to be a matter of degree, and they were not clear to the American voters.

At the polls in November Willkie lost to Franklin Roosevelt by nearly five million ballots. He polled more popular votes than any Republican candidate up to 1940, but he garnered only eighty-two electoral votes from ten states. It was generally agreed at the time that the most significant influences on the election were the frightening international situation and the traditional class voting patterns that had existed before the campaign began.

After the election, Willkie pledged his "loyal opposition" to the President and worked for more aid to Britain. In implementing these goals, he gradually alienated certain members of the Old Guard within the G.O.P. He took a trip to England to observe the war effort, and came back firmly committed to the Administration's lend-lease program of assistance to all opponents of Hitler. This proposal for involvement offended other Republicans, and gradually civil war broke out within the party. The Willkie supporters became more internationalist while his foes became more anti-interventionist and increasingly critical of their titular head. On November 2, 1941, for example, a group of House Republicans actively organized an effort to read Wendell Willkie out of the Republican party because of his attempt "to involve this country in an undeclared war." Willkie countered by demanding that the G.O.P. purge itself of isolationists. Later in the month, when the repeal of the Neutrality Act of 1939 came up for a vote, less than 12 per cent of the congressional Republicans were willing to follow Willkie's demand for repeal and a more aggressive policy against Germany. When Pearl Harbor was bombed and America entered the war, all partisan forces united, but scars remained and Willkie's leadership of the Republicans was never again fully accepted by all of the factions within the party.

In 1942, in spite of urging by his friends, Willkie decided

not to run against Dewey for the governship of New York. Instead, he continued to work for what he called "an enlightened foreign policy." On August 26, as a personal representative of the President, he left the United States for his trip around the world described in this volume. Next to the campaign of 1940, the "one world" trip was the most dramatic event of Willkie's life. It publicized many issues of the war and attracted worldwide attention to the cooperation existing between the heads of America's rival parties.

Willkie was away forty-nine days and his travels made daily news from all around the world. His recommendations concerning military strategy, aims and objectives, and policies of the United States often irritated Administration decision-makers and caused comments among governmental leaders throughout the flaming globe. Because he had not been informed of the forthcoming North African invasion, he called for a "second front" in both Moscow and China. The comments were bewildering, for it was impossible for allied leaders to know when Willkie was acting for Roosevelt and when he was speaking as an American tourist. When Willkie heard of the confusion, he said: "I speak for no one else and no one else speaks for me. When I speak for myself I'm Wendell Willkie and I say what I damn please." The situation was exaggerated when President Roosevelt told correspondents that he had read the headlines concerning Willkie's appeal for a second front, but he had not thought it worthwhile to read the news stories himself. A number of reporters had drawn the clear impression from Roosevelt that he was irritated by Willkie's blunt appeal, and they wrote that he had disavowed Willkie as his personal representative. In a subsequent interview, however, the President declined to comment on Willkie's remarks, saying that any controversy was merely political. He said that everything was all right with the Willkie mission as far as he was concerned. Nevertheless, on October 12, in a speech discussing manpower and other issues, including the drafting of eighteen-year-olds, the President said: "I can say one thing about these plans of ours; they are not being decided by the typewriter strategists who expound their views in the press or on the radio. . . . The trouble with the typewriter strategists is that, while they may be full of bright ideas, they are not in possession of much information about the facts or the problems of military operations. We therefore will continue to leave the plans for this war to the military leaders."

Whether these remarks were aimed at Willkie is not known, but he thought that they were and he became very angry. When Willkie was about to return to the United States, Stephen Early, Roosevelt's secretary, contacted Mr. Samuel Pryor, prominent Connecticut Republican and close friend of Willkie, and asked him to have the 1940 candidate stop in Washington to report to the President. Willkie did this, issuing a statement that he had told the President "very frankly and candidly" of the things he had seen and heard during his trip through fourteen countries, and that his proposals had been made only after talking with high-ranking officers of the United States, Britain, and Russia. He also told the reporters that "Mr. Roosevelt had volunteered the statement that any reports that he had 'criticized' me or my activities while abroad were entirely erroneous."

According to Pryor, this was an understatement. Pryor declared: "Willkie saw the President and they thrashed things out that night. Willkie really raised hell with Roosevelt. No one ever talked to 'F.D.R.' like Willkie did that night. This explains why Roosevelt was so cool concerning the trip when he reported to the press." In any event, Willkie had made the trip and a number of analysts found the response favorable. He had exercised his opportunity to criticize major policies while acting as Roosevelt's representative, and he had gathered public opinion behind his more vigorous prosecution of the war. On October 26 he made a nationwide broadcast concerning his tour of the world. Speaking to an estimated thirty-six million persons, he renewed his demand for a second front in Europe, expressed hope that an offensive would be undertaken in Burma, and warned the American people that the United States stood to lose half its friends abroad if it did not begin to do a more satisfactory job on the war. He declared that he had made the journey as a free agent and had become convinced that the world was so small that a Pacific charter and global planning were vital to the future. He asserted to his vast audience: "Winning the war is not enough. . . . To win the peace, three things seem to be necessary: first, we must plan for peace on a global basis; second, the world must be free, economically and politically, for nations and for men that peace may exist in it; third, America must play an active,

xiv

a constructive part in freeing it and in keeping its peace." Finally, Willkie also spoke of freedom for colonial countries, American efforts in the war, and his observations of the countries he had visited.

The strong statement, like so many of his speeches, prompted all types of response. The huge personal mail Willkie received was overwhelmingly favorable, and the President, when questioned about the talk, said, "there is not a controversy [between us] in a car load of speeches." Many other Democrats endorsed parts of the address, but most Republican congressmen were only lukewarm toward it. Willkie again had provided national stimulation to postwar planning before millions of listeners, but, as in the past, his work did little to advance his leadership within his own party's ranks.

Many of Willkie's observations after his trip were reiterated and refined in *One World*. His theme was a plea for coexistence with Communists on the one hand and a strengthening of democracy on the other. Willkie noted the need for intellectual exchange with all nations because he worried about the lack of understanding of the United States by underprivileged nations. He observed the dread of foreign control felt by many peoples, and predicted a weakening of the colonial systems throughout the world. He detected the paradox of increased nationalism with the postwar necessity for cooperation. He seems to have anticipated the current revolutions based on rising expectations in many small countries and he hoped that they would be compatible with the aspirations for common security among all nations.

But it must be kept in mind that Willkie wrote and thought in the terms and resources of 1943. Russia and China were then allies; Germany and Japan were the enemies. These roles are now reversed. People and situations on the world scene have changed, and so some of the chapters are out of date. Willkie was wrong about Chou En-lai and the agrarian awakening but he was right about China's determination to shake off the past. Nevertheless, there is much of value in Willkie's discussion of poverty, public health, liberty, and social dignity among underdeveloped nations. And as we read Willkie's thoughts about the world of 1943, we can observe several parallels to our beleagured globe of more than two decades later.

With reference to domestic matters, Willkie's remarks are almost as appropriate as they were a generation ago. When he wrote of race imperialism [p. 190] in the United States or of an overzealous mass insistence upon general conformity to majority standards [p. 191] and the revival of age-old racial and religious distrusts, he hit sensitive spots that remain sensitive today. His words on the importance of minorities within a democracy [pp. 194-195] are among his most enduring phrases. If the Republican party had heeded the implications of Willkie's admonitions after World War II, and had really stressed acceptance of minority groups, the G.O.P. would have been more successful in recent elections.

For the most part *One World* jelled some thoughts and created some controversy. Willkie's popularity among the general citizenry went up; within the party it took another dip. This was partly because the "one world" trip was taken during the campaign of 1942, and Willkie thus did little to assist the party's candidates running for office in November. It was also due to the fact that Willkie traveled as Roosevelt's representative, and that the book contained blunt statements that still rubbed raw on certain interests in the G.O.P. who were not as committed to internationalism as both the 1940 standard bearers. To many Republican professionals, Willkie's uncompromising devotion to the international scene and his critical lack of interest in basic party activities disqualified him from serious reconsideration in 1944. He became leader of an ever decreasing faction of liberals within the party, and when he tried to recapture the nomination, he discovered that much of his party support at the local level had evaporated. Willkie had been not only the liberal-wing leader but also an aggravating critic. The conservatives found it impossible to accept him and the moderates thought him too controversial when compared to Governor Dewey, who was available. Willkie was soundly defeated in the Wisconsin presidential preference primary election in April, 1944, and promptly withdrew his candidacy for the nomination.

During the following summer he wrote a series of articles with which he hoped to influence the Republican delegates and the American voters. On topics such as Federal Power and States' Rights, The American Negro, Social Security, Labor and International Trade, he presented his final thoughts in powerful and principled prose that indicated how far ahead of his party he was thinking. But there is little indication that his ideas were accepted at the convention. As a new candidate became the party leader, his platform and his policies had to be given priority.

Willkie did not participate in the campaign of 1944, and he had endorsed neither Dewey nor Roosevelt before he had a series of heart attacks in August and September of that year. He died in New York on October 8, 1944.

Willkie's world, "one in integrity," was short-lived after World War II. The international organizatioṅ about which he dreamed came into existence, but the unified world of free and democratic people that was the foundation of the dreams disintegrated gradually as the forces of nationalism were resurrected over the earth. That is one of the reasons why Willkie's discussion of democracy and freedom and hope in *One World* still makes, with a little imagination and reflection, interesting and valuable reading for this new era.

TO

MAJOR RICHARD T. KIGHT, D.F.C.,
who piloted The Gulliver, the plane in which we flew
around the world, and to whom on November 24, 1942,
the War Department awarded the Oak Leaf Cluster for
extraordinary achievement in completing that "difficult
and hazardous mission in excellent time and without
mishap, despite extreme weather conditions and the
presence of enemy aircraft over
part of the route,"

AND TO

the members of the tireless and skillful crew of
The Gulliver,
CAPTAIN ALEXIS KLOTZ, CO-PILOT
CAPTAIN JOHN C. WAGNER
MASTER SERGEANT JAMES M. COOPER
TECHNICAL SERGEANT RICHARD J. BARRETT
SERGEANT VICTOR P. MINKOFF
CORPORAL CHARLES H. REYNOLDS

The author wishes to express his thanks to the editors of the Readers Digest, The New York Times Sunday Magazine, the Saturday Evening Post, and Look for permission to use, in three of the chapters of this book, excerpts from articles which he wrote for these magazines.

TABLE OF CONTENTS

INTRODUCTION

TODAY, because of military and other censorships, America is like a beleaguered city that lives within high walls through which there passes only an occasional courier to tell us what is happening outside. I have been outside those walls. And I have found that nothing outside is exactly what it seems to those within.

I had an opportunity to fly around the world in the middle of this war, to see and talk to hundreds of people in more than a dozen nations, and to talk intimately with many of the world's leaders. It was an experience which few private citizens and none of those leaders have had. It gave me some new and urgent convictions and strengthened some of my old ones. These convictions are not mere humanitarian hopes; they are not just idealistic and vague. They are based on things I saw and learned at first hand and upon the views of men and women, important and anonymous, whose heroism and sacrifices give meaning and life to their beliefs.

In this book I have tried to set down as dispassionately as possible some of my observations and—perhaps not quite so dispassionately—the conclusions I have drawn from them.

I was accompanied on my trip by Gardner (Mike) Cowles, Jr., a noted publisher, and by Joseph Barnes, an experienced foreign correspondent and editor—both perfect traveling companions, both my friends. They have been most generous and helpful in the preparation of material for this book. And though I am sure they would agree with many of my conclusions, they bear no responsibility for this expression of them.

Captain Paul Pihl, U. S. Navy, and Major Grant Mason, U. S. Army, went with me as representatives of those services and gave me valuable advice on the trip from their special knowledge. Everyone in the party and crew alike was helpful and companionable. But I know I am gratifying the wish of all when I pay special tribute to Major Richard (Dick) Kight, our equitable, engaging pilot, for his amazing skill in the operation of the bomber in which we flew.

W. L. W.

New York
March 2, 1943

ONE
WORLD

1

El Alamein

IN A four-engined Consolidated bomber, converted for transport service and operated by United States Army officers, I left Mitchel Field, New York, on August 26, to see what I could of the world and the war, its battle fronts, its leaders, and its people. Exactly forty-nine days later, on October 14, I landed in Minneapolis, Minnesota. I had encircled the world, not in the northern latitudes where the circumference is small, but on a route which crossed the equator twice.

I had traveled a total of 31,000 miles, which—looked at as a figure—still impresses and almost bewilders me. For the net impression of my trip was not one of distance from other peoples, but of closeness to them. If I had ever had any doubts that the world has become small and completely interdependent, this trip would have dispelled them altogether.

The extraordinary fact is that to cover this enormous dis-

tance we were in the air a total of only 160 hours. We usually flew from eight to ten hours a day when we were on
the move, which means that out of the forty-nine days given
to the trip, I had about thirty days on the ground for the
accomplishment of the purposes in hand. The physical business of moving from one country to another, or from one
continent to another, was no more arduous than the trips
an American businessman may make any day of his life to
carry on his business. In fact, moving about the world came
to seem so easy that I promised the president of a great central Siberian republic to fly back some week end in 1945
for a day's hunting. And I expect to keep the engagement.

There are no distant points in the world any longer. I
learned by this trip that the myriad millions of human
beings of the Far East are as close to us as Los Angeles is
to New York by the fastest trains. I cannot escape the conviction that in the future what concerns them must concern
us, almost as much as the problems of the people of California concern the people of New York.

Our thinking in the future must be world-wide.

On the way to Cairo, at the end of August, bad news
came to meet us. At Kano, Nigeria, there was open speculation as to how many days it might take General Rommel
to cover the few miles which lay between his advance scouts
and Alexandria. By the time we reached Khartoum, this
speculation had become hard reports of what is known in
Egypt as a "flap"—a mild form of panic. In Cairo, some
Europeans were packing cars for flight southward or east-

ward. I recalled the President's warning to me just before I left Washington that before I reached Cairo it might well be in German hands. We heard tales of Nazi parachutists dropped in the Nile Valley to disorganize its last defenses. The British Eighth Army was widely believed to be preparing to evacuate Egypt altogether, retiring to Palestine and southward into the Sudan and Kenya.

Naturally, I wanted to check these reports. And Cairo itself was the world's worst place to check anything. There were good men there. Alexander Kirk, United States Minister to Egypt, was not hopeful about the future, but I learned from my long talks with him that he used his corrosive, cynical pessimism as a mask to cover what was really extensive knowledge of what was going on and great skill in trying to hold a fragile situation together. There were other well-informed men in Cairo, not least among them the round, laughing Prime Minister, Nahas Pasha, who has so much gusto and good humor that I told him if he would come to the United States and run for office, he would undoubtedly make a formidable candidate.

But the city was full of rumors and alarms. The streets were filled with officers and soldiers coming and going. A very tight censorship made the American reporters in Cairo doubt and feel skeptical of all British reports from the front. In a half-hour at Shepheard's Hotel, you could pick up a dozen different versions of what was taking place in the desert not much more than a hundred miles away.

So I accepted eagerly an invitation from General Sir Bernard L. Montgomery to see the front for myself, at El Alamein. With Mike Cowles and Major General Russell L. Maxwell, then commander of United States forces in Egypt, we drove out of Cairo on the desert road to the front. I had bought, at a French department store in Cairo, a khaki shirt and trousers, both several sizes too small for me, but the best they had, and we borrowed the simple bedding which every man carries with him in desert fighting.

General Montgomery met me at his headquarters, hidden among sand dunes on the Mediterranean. In fact, it was so near the beach that he and General Alexander and I took our next morning's bath in those marvelous blue-green waters. Headquarters consisted of four American automobile trailers spaced a few dozen yards apart against the dunes for concealment purposes. In one of these, the general had his maps and battle plans. He gave me one for sleeping quarters. In another his aide put up and in the fourth the general himself lived, when he was not at the front.

This was not often. The wiry, scholarly, intense, almost fanatical personality of General Montgomery made a deep impression on me when I was in Egypt, but no part of his character was more remarkable than his passionate addiction to work. He was almost never in Cairo. He was usually at the front itself, with his men. I was surprised to find that he did not even know General Maxwell, who had been in complete charge of American forces in the Middle East for several weeks. When we drove up to his headquarters he took me aside and asked, "Who is that officer with you?" I replied, "General Maxwell." And he went on, "Who's General Maxwell?" I had just finished explaining when General Maxwell himself approached and I introduced the two.

Almost before we were out of our cars, General Montgomery launched into a detailed description of a battle which was in its last phases and which for the first time in months had stopped Rommel dead. No real news of this battle had reached Cairo or had been given to the press. The general repeated the details for us step by step, telling us exactly what had happened and why he felt it was a major victory even though his forces had not advanced any great distance. It had been a testing of strength on a heavy scale. Had the British lost, Rommel would have been in Cairo in a few days.

It was my first lesson in the strategy and tactics of desert warfare, in which distance means nothing and mobility and fire power are everything. At first it was hard for me to understand why the general kept repeating, in a quiet way, "Egypt has been saved." The enemy was deep in Egypt and had not retreated. I remembered the skepticism I had found in Cairo, born of earlier British claims. But before I left the trailer in which General Montgomery had rigged up his map room, I had learned more about desert warfare, and he had convinced me that something more than the ubiquitous self-confidence of the British officer and gentleman lay behind his assurance that the threat to Egypt had been liquidated.

General Montgomery spoke with great enthusiasm of the American-manufactured General Sherman tanks, which were just then beginning to arrive in important numbers on the docks at Alexandria and Port Said. He also spoke very highly of the 105-millimeter self-propelled antitank cannon of American make, which was just then beginning to prove that a tank *can* be stopped.

Almost his central thesis was his belief that earlier British reverses on the desert front had resulted from inadequate co-ordination of tank forces, artillery forces, and air power. General Montgomery told me he had his air officer living with him at his headquarters, and that complete co-ordination of planes, tanks, and artillery had been chiefly responsible for the decisive check to Rommel of the last few days. He estimated that the Germans had lost some 140 tanks, about half of them high-quality tanks, in the battle just about concluded, against a British loss of only 37 tanks; and he predicted that he would achieve the same supremacy on the ground that he already had in the air.

That evening, we had dinner in General Montgomery's tent with his superior officer, General Sir Harold R. L. G. Alexander, commander of all British forces in the Middle East, General Maxwell, Major General Lewis H. Brereton, then commanding American air forces in the Middle East, and his British counterpart, Air Marshal Sir Arthur Tedder. Air Marshal Tedder, whom I had also seen and talked with in Cairo, is a curiously charming and impressive soldier, with soft, quiet face and voice, who carries water colors with him on every assignment into the desert. He is a flying hero, and a thoughtful man.

Brereton and Tedder talked that night about the future of the campaign, and nothing that has happened since has

6

made their talk seem bold or boasting. They were both convinced of the possibility of reopening the Mediterranean to United Nations shipping. They agreed that this could happen only after Rommel had been driven back west of the Bengasi bulge. Then, they said, we could again provision and garrison our forces in Egypt and farther east along shipping lanes which would hug the African coast under successive umbrellas of fighting aircraft based on Gibraltar, on Malta, on Bengasi, and on the huge United States air bases in Palestine. They also talked of large-scale bombing of Italy as a real possibility if they held the Bengasi region.

The conversation ranged over many subjects, one of the officers even explaining to me that in the British Army a latrine was irreverently called "The House of Lords." But General Montgomery did not want to talk much about anything except the front. He would listen politely to other talk and within a minute or two swing the conversation back to desert fighting. However, later, he and I walked from his mess tent over to my sleeping quarters. He made sure that my bunk was in order and then we sat on the steps of the trailer, from which we could see whitecaps breaking on the sea under the moon and hear at our backs in the distance the pounding of his artillery against Rommel's withdrawing forces. He was in a reminiscent and reflective mood and talked of his boyhood days in County Donegal, of his long years in the British Army, with service in many parts of the world, of his continuous struggle since the war began to infuse both public officials and Army officers with the necessity for an affirmative instead of a defensive attitude.

"I tell you, Willkie, it's the only way we will defeat the Boches"—he always spoke of the Germans as "the Boches." "Give them no rest, give them no rest. These Boches are good soldiers. They are professionals."

When I asked him about Rommel, he said, "He's a trained, skilled general. But he has one weakness. He repeats his tactics. And that's the way I'm going to get him."

He got up to go, wishing me a good rest, and saying, "I always read a bit before I turn in." And then a little sadly he told me that he had a few books with him. In fact, that everything he had in the world was with him. A short while before he left England he had stored his furnishings and his books, the collection of a lifetime, in a warehouse at Dover. "The Boches in a raid destroyed the warehouse," he added.

The next day we toured the front and I saw with my own eyes the clusters of tank and artillery troops, the occasional fighter-plane bases, and the formidable supply units which constitute a front in the fluid, checkerboard type of warfare that goes on in the desert. Again I was enormously impressed by the depth and thoroughness of General Montgomery's knowledge of his business. Whether it was corps or division, brigade, regiment, or battalion headquarters, he knew more in detail of the deployment of the troops and location of the tanks than did the officer in charge. This may sound extravagant but it was literally true. The man's passion for detail is amazing.

We inspected dozens of German tanks scattered over the desert. They had been captured by the British and blown up at Montgomery's orders. As we would climb up on these wrecked tanks, he would open the food boxes and hand to me the charred remnants of British provisions and supplies which the Germans had taken when they captured Tobruk. "You see, Willkie, the devils have been living on us. But they are not going to do it again. At least they are never going to use these tanks against us again."

All the while we were going over the front, the British artillery was thundering steadily and British and American aircraft were harassing Rommel's retreating troops. The Germans, in retaliation, were sending squadrons of Stuttgart planes in quick, sharp strafing raids against British artillery positions. Here and there above us, we would see in the bright sky a plane that had been hit spinning to the earth in a spiral of fire and smoke and occasionally we'd see the floating parachutes of the pilots who had been lucky enough to get out in time—all of them floating, it seemed to me, out over the Mediterranean, under the propulsion of a gentle breeze from the south.

Among the soldiers we saw at the front were Englishmen, Australians, New Zealanders, Canadians, South Africans, and a company of about thirty Americans. The last were a small tank corps which had been sent by air from the United States for training in actual battle conditions. I talked with each of the Americans and found that they represented eighteen different states. They seemed well and were frank about their desire to get back to the United States and they plied me with eager questions about the Dodgers and the Cardinals, who were then in the final race for the pennant. These men had just come out of the fighting and expected to go back in an hour. But there were no heroics, no big talk. They were just a group of physically hard, alert American boys who were wondering when they'd next see Texas, Broadway, and the Iowa farm.

At noon we stopped for lunch at the headquarters of a divisional commander, another group of automobile trailers. The lunch was sandwiches—and flies. At the front, the flies annoyed the soldiers almost as much as the Germans did. They get into your mouth and ears and nose. They are an irritation peculiar to desert warfare but as real, I should judge, as the mud of the trenches in France. Many of the officers also complained of the fine sand blowing constantly into their eyes and skin. It causes tremendous wear on all mechanical equipment, too. One flier told me that the usual types of airplane engine last only twenty-five per cent of normal expectancy in desert conditions, and everywhere I went in Egypt I found top-notch British and American air engineers talking about the intricacies of filters.

On the way back to General Montgomery's headquarters, he summed up what I had seen and heard. He minced no words at all in describing his situation as excellent, and the battle just concluded as a victory of decisive significance.

"With the superiority in tanks and planes that I have established as a result of this battle and with Rommel's inability to get reinforcements of matériel across the eastern Mediterranean—for our air forces are destroying four out of every five of his matériel transports—it is now mathematically certain that I will eventually destroy Rommel. This battle was the critical test."

I had seen his operating figures on his own and the enemy's tank losses and tank reserves. Many of the enemy's losses I had also seen with my own eyes. He affirmed the information I had been given earlier about the supplies that were even then being unloaded from American ships east of Alexandria.

And he asked a favor of me. He said that a spirit of defeatism permeated Egypt, North Africa, and the Middle East; that successive British failures had led many to believe that the Germans were going to capture Egypt. That because of this, Great Britain had lost prestige. And this loss interfered with his secret service and helped the enemy's. He had stopped Rommel but he was anxious for him not to begin to retreat into the desert before some three hundred American General Sherman tanks that had just landed at Port Said could get into action. He estimated this would take about three weeks. He figured that if he made a formal public announcement of the result of the battle, Rommel's withdrawal might be hastened. But he thought that an unofficial statement made by me would not be regarded by Rommel as a sign of aggressive action on his part, while at the same time it would have an even greater effect than a formal British communiqué in stiffening the morale of Egypt and Africa and the Middle East.

I was convinced from all I had seen and heard that he was not overestimating the importance of what he had accomplished and I was glad to do as he wished.

He accordingly called the representatives of the press to his headquarters, and I told them the results of the battle in the language which he and I had agreed upon in advance: "Egypt is saved. Rommel is stopped and a beginning has been made on the task of throwing the Nazis out of Africa."

It was the first good news from the British side that these newspapermen had had in a long time. They had been fooled many times and were wary. The battle line, to their eyes, had hardly sagged, Rommel was still only a few miles from the Nile, while the road to Tripoli, from where we were, seemed long and a little fanciful and the road to Cairo painfully short.

I saw in the faces of many of the reporters that afternoon a polite sort of skepticism. They had grown accustomed to generals who predict. They had had no experience with generals who perform.

From Montgomery's headquarters I flew in a little German scout plane, its cabin constructed almost entirely of glass so that one could see in all directions, low over the battlefield to the American and British air base. Air Marshal Tedder piloted the plane.

We saw, at the base, hundreds of American and British aviators, some just returned from fighting, some just taking off. Others sat about exchanging experiences, discussing the wind and the weather, all quite nonchalant. I inquired with some concern about the probable fate of the boys I had seen that morning floating with their parachutes toward the Mediterranean. They could not be identified, but the officer in charge said: "It's surprising how many of them drift back. Some fall behind enemy lines, some into the sea, and some far into the desert. But their ingenuity and self-reliance bring an amazing number of them back to headquarters."

After talking with a number of the American fliers, whom I found in much the same mood as the American soldiers I had seen on the desert, the Air Marshal and I flew on to Alexandria. This was an interlude which served to remind me that all this war is not so direct, so hard, and so essentially simple as the sand or the tanks or the long, clean gun barrels I had been looking at.

Two memories stand out in my mind today of Alexandria. The first was a long discussion with Rear Admiral René Godfroy, in command of the forlorn units of the French fleet in the harbor. His ships were visible from all over town. Their breechblocks were on the shore, their hulls were covered with barnacles, they had oil for only a short run. But still they represented an important potential striking power. And their presence there, great machines of death into which French peasants had poured their savings and French engineers and sailors their skill, useless, crippled and without honor while France was still enslaved by the Nazis, was a tragic reminder that this war was still a confused and dirty business in which too many men and groups have not yet chosen sides.

Admiral Godfroy spoke good English. He impressed me as a high-grade, competent French officer, and the British officers who had introduced me to him confirmed my impression. He was sorely troubled by the turn of events in France, and almost uneducated in any meaning of the war outside his simple officer's discipline. He had obviously been deeply embittered by the naval actions of the British against French ships after June, 1940. But he expressed great friendship for the United States and a desire for our victory. Although, he said, he took his orders only from Marshal Pétain so long as the Marshal was alive, it was obvious from what he said to me about his own feelings, as well as the feelings of his sailors, that he hoped that American forces would come, and he gave me every indication that if they did the resistance of his fleet would be only a token one.

Since my talk with him and with other French officers, sailors, and soldiers in North Africa, I have never accepted without discount stories of the probable losses we would have sustained at the hands of the French if we had gone in directly as Americans without dealing with Darlan. I have always suspected tales that can be neither proved nor disproved and which too aptly support a political policy.

My second memory of Alexandria is of a dinner that night at the home of Admiral Harwood, hero of the epic fight of the *Exeter* against the *Graf Spee* in South American waters, and now commander of the British Navy in the eastern Mediterranean. He invited to dine with us ten of his compatriots in the naval, diplomatic, or consular service in Alexandria. We discussed the war in the detached, almost impersonal way in which the war is discussed all over the world by officers engaged in fighting it, and then the conversation turned to politics. I tried to draw out these men, all of them experienced and able administrators of the British Empire, on what they saw in the future, and especially in the future

14

of the colonial system and of our joint relations with the many peoples of the East.

What I got was Rudyard Kipling, untainted even with the liberalism of Cecil Rhodes. I knew that informed Englishmen in London and all over the British Commonwealth were working hard on these problems, that many of them, for example, were trying to find a formula which will go farther toward self-government than the older concept of "trusteeship." But these men, executing the policies made in London, had no idea that the world was changing. The British colonial system was not perfect in their eyes; it seemed to me simply that no one of them had ever thought of it as anything that might possibly be changed or modified in any way. The Atlantic Charter most of them had read about. That it might affect their careers or their thinking had never occurred to any of them. That evening started in my mind a conviction which was to grow strong in the days that followed it in the Middle East: that brilliant victories in the field will not win for us this war now going on in the far reaches of the world, that only new men and new ideas in the machinery of our relations with the peoples of the East can win the victory without which any peace will be only another armistice.

Next day we drove back to Cairo for long conferences with King Farouk, the Prime Minister, and later with Sir Miles Lampson, the British Ambassador to Egypt, and, for all practical purposes, its actual ruler. All along the way we passed through a strange medley of the ancient and the modern. Long camel trains with their native riders streamed by loaded with products of the Nile Valley, and rows of modern trucks hauled back to Cairo high-powered modern fighting planes to be repaired in modern machine shops—and always in the distance we could see those reminders of ancient Egyptian glory, the Sphinx and the pyramids.

2

The Middle East

FROM CAIRO TO TEHERAN, we flew above trade routes and over cities which are as old as anything in our civilization and which have kept the variety and the contrasts of thousands of years of history. The blindfolded water buffaloes walking in endless circles around irrigation pumps in the valley of the Nile seemed at the time to have little to do with the great American repair depots I saw in Egypt. Underfed and scrawny children playing in the dirty streets of the old city at Jerusalem, young French cadets on the airfield at Beirut, Arab boys and girls of ten working in a blanket factory in Bagdad, Polish refugees camped in great barracks outside Teheran—the first picture I had of this region we call the Middle East was one of contrasts, sharp colors, and confusion.

In the air, between stops, an airplane gives a modern traveler a chance to map in his mind the land he is flying over. From Beirut to Lydda, to Bagdad, to Teheran, we had fairly long flights on which to compare notes and to sort out impressions. Before we left Iran for the Soviet Union, I had made up my own mind about the answers to some of the most immediate and pressing questions I had asked myself about the Middle East.

In the first place, I was convinced that all these peoples were more on our side than against us. Partly, this was simply because America was far away and not exercising any control over them. These are important reasons, by the way, for such popularity as the Germans still enjoy—in Iran, for example. In addition, America's entry into the war had convinced large numbers that whatever might be the temporary setbacks, the United Nations would eventually win. In other words, these peoples of the Middle East who have been overrun by successive conquerors since before the days of Alexander the Great have a large element of the purely practical in their thinking and an instinct for survival that leads them to pick the winning side before the conclusion becomes obvious.

In the second place, I was convinced that some sort of yeast was at work in nearly all the places I visited. Even the strictest kind of neutrality cannot keep the war from working its profound and violent changes on all the peoples who live in this region. Their lives will change more in the next ten years than they have in the last ten centuries.

In the third place, I found no automatic guarantee that these changes will be in our favor. The magic of our Western political ideas has been sharply challenged in the minds of many Moslems, many Arabs, many Jews, many Iranians.

18

They have watched us now at close range, for almost a generation, while we have been fighting each other and ourselves and questioning the central structure of our own beliefs. Everywhere I found polite but skeptical people, who met my questions about their problems and difficulties with polite but ironic questions about our own. The maladjustments of races in America came up frequently, and I believe every government official I talked to wondered about our relations to Vichy. Arab and Jew were curious to know if our expressions of freedom meant only new and enlarged mandated areas which in the Lebanon and Syria and Palestine, rightly or wrongly, had come to mean to them a form of foreign tyranny.

Finally, everywhere I went in the Middle East I found a kind of technological backwardness along with poverty and squalor. Any American who makes this comment lays himself open, I realize, to the charge of being overconscious of bathtubs. But I understood in Jerusalem for the first time how so many other Americans have gone there with a real feeling of returning to Biblical times. The reason was that they were in truth returning to Biblical times, where little has changed in two thousand years. Modern airlines, oil pipe lines, macadam streets, or even plumbing constitute a thin veneer on the surface of a life which in essence is as simple and as hard as it was before there was any West. The only major exceptions to this one finds in the developments, industrial, agricultural, and cultural, which have been made under the supervision of the world Zionist movement or where the Arabs have, as in Bagdad, achieved a measure of self-government.

Four things, it seemed to me, these peoples need, in varying degree and in different ways. They need more education. They need more public-health work. They need more modern industry. And they need more of the social dignity and self-confidence which come from freedom and self-rule.

No one can travel down the Nile, I believe, even when it is the backdrop to a war, without realizing what education could do to help restore to the Egyptian people the national virility that history itself claims for them. The country has started schools; Americans and English have helped; I met Egyptians, from King Farouk and the Prime Minister, Nahas Pasha, to engineers and doctors, who would be recognized as educated men anywhere. Yet nowhere in Egypt—or in the whole Middle East, for that matter, except in Turkey—did anyone suggest showing me a native school as a matter of national pride. The only school that anyone urged me to see was a girls' school operated by an American woman who, under great discouragement, had been attempting to teach Egyptian orphans for thirty years.

I met pashas at every reception I went to. Many of them are married to foreign wives; they are socially attractive, genial men. Public squares are filled with statues of them. "Pasha" is a title which has survived in Egypt from Ottoman times. It was formerly a rank conferred on military leaders or provincial governors who served the empire well. Now it has become a courtesy title, bestowed by the king. Egyptian people figuratively and literally roll out the red carpet for a pasha whenever he appears, for he has the money with which to hire such services.

But when I asked one of my hosts, a young Egyptian newspaperman, "Does a man become a pasha by writing a great book?" he answered, "I suppose he could, except that almost no one in Egypt writes books."

"Do you get to be a pasha by painting pictures?" I asked.

"There is no reason why you couldn't, except that no one here paints pictures."

"Does a great inventor ever get to be a pasha?" And I was told once more, "We've had no great inventors that I know of since the time of the Pharaohs."

I was not in Egypt long enough to learn all the reasons for this cultural sterility. The fact that culture and education in Egypt's great cosmopolitan city of Cairo are dominated by non-Egyptians has something to do with it; as does the predominant ownership of Egypt's fertile land by a small group of pashas who, for the most part, have attained their titles not even by political activities but through the use of their wealth.

But the major reason seemed to be the complete absence of a middle class. Throughout the Middle East there is a small percentage of wealthy landowners whose property is largely hereditary. I met a number of them and found them largely disinterested in any political movement, except as it affected the perpetuation of their own status. The great mass of the people, outside of the roaming tribes, are impoverished, own no property, are hideously ruled by the practices of ancient priestcraft, and are living in conditions of squalor.

The urge and the strength to create do not come, as a rule, from those who have too much or from those who have nothing. In the Middle East there is little in between.

Yet, strange as it may seem, one senses a ferment in these lands, a groping of the long-inert masses, a growing disregard of restrictive religious rites and practices. In every city I found a group—usually a small group—of restless, energetic, intellectual young people who knew the techniques of the mass movement that had brought about the revolution in Russia and talked about them. They knew also the history of our own democratic development. In their talk with me they seemed to be weighing in their minds the course through which their own intense, almost fanatical, aspirations should be achieved. Likewise I found in this part of the world, as I found in Russia, in China, everywhere, a growing spirit of fervid nationalism, a disturbing thing to one who believes that the only hope of the world lies in the opposite trend.

I found much the same discontent, hunger, and impatience in Iraq, in the Lebanon, in Iran, and much the same time lag in official recognition of the problem, though the Prime and Foreign Ministers of those countries are knowing and able men.

In Beirut, in Teheran, and in Cairo, Americans have begun to help by founding and maintaining schools open to everyone. In Beirut, I drank tea with Bayard Dodge, president of the American University of Beirut, in his garden. That same day, I had met General Charles de Gaulle, leader of the Fighting French, General Georges Catroux, their

Delegate General, and Major General Edward Louis Spears, the British Minister, and had talked with each of them about the future of Syria and the Lebanon. But it is no exaggeration to say that Dr. Dodge gave me more hope and confidence for the future of those regions than all the others combined.

I shall, however, never forget my visit with General de Gaulle. I was met at the airport at Beirut, received by an elaborately uniformed color guard and band, and whisked several miles to the house where the general was living—a great white structure, surrounded by elaborate and formal gardens, where guards saluted at every turn. We talked for hours in the general's private room, where every corner, every wall, held busts, statues, and pictures of Napoleon. The conversation continued through an elaborate dinner and went on late into the night, as we sat out on a beautiful starlit lawn.

Frequently the general, in describing his struggle of the moment with the British as to whether he or they should dominate Syria and the Lebanon, would declare dramatically, "I cannot sacrifice or compromise my principles." "Like Joan of Arc," his aide added. When I referred to my great interest in the Fighting French movement, he corrected me sharply. "The Fighting French are not a movement. The Fighting French are France itself. We are the residuary legatees of all of France and its possessions." When I reminded him that Syria was but a mandated area under the League of Nations, he said, "Yes, I know. But I hold it in trust. I cannot close out that mandate or let anyone else do so. That can be done only when there is a government again in France. In no place in this world can I yield a single French right, though I am perfectly willing to sit with Winston Churchill and Franklin Roosevelt and consider ways and means by which French rights and French territories can be momentarily and temporarily used in order to help drive the Germans and the collaborators from the control of France.

"Mr. Willkie," he continued, "some people forget that I and my associates represent France. They apparently do not have in mind France's glorious history. They are thinking in terms of its momentary eclipse."

Later I was talking with one of the high officials of the Lebanon about the struggle that was then going on between the French and the British for the control of Syria and the Middle East. I asked him where his sympathies lay, and he replied, "A plague on both their houses." The intellectual leaven in the Middle East has little faith in a system of mandates and colonies, whatever power controls.

From Beirut I went on to Jerusalem. Never was the contrast between old and new more dramatic. For from the windows of our modern, smoothly, swiftly flying plane we could look down through the clear air upon the hills where once stood the cedars of Lebanon, upon the Dead Sea, the Sea of Galilee, the river Jordan, the Mount of Olives, and the Garden of Gethsemane.

In Jerusalem I was the guest of Sir Harold MacMichael, the athletic, pipe-smoking, very able and very British Resident High Commissioner for Palestine and Trans-Jordan.

He showed me the old city and explained with infinite patience and good humor the distinctions an American finds it hard to see between a colony and a mandated area.

But it was Lowell C. Pinkerton, American Consul General at Jerusalem, who arranged for me to see at first hand the real intricacies of the problems of Palestine. Through his hospitable house, he ushered in order representatives of all the conflicting factions of Jews and Arabs, and for one crowded day Joe Barnes and Mike Cowles and I interviewed them. Major General D. F. McConnel, commander of British forces in the area, came in, and Robert Scott, acting chief secretary of Sir Harold's administration; able and understanding Moshe Shertok, head of the political department of the Jewish Agency, and Ruhi Bey Abdul Hadi, Arab member of Sir Harold's secretariat; Dr. Arieh Altman, head of the Revisionist faction of Zionism which claims the entire country for the Jews; and Awni Bey Abdul Hadi, Arab lawyer and nationalist leader who claims the whole country for the Arabs. All told us their stories.

By the end of the day, I felt a great temptation to conclude that the only solution of this tangled problem must be as drastic as Solomon's. But then I went to call on Miss Henrietta Szold, founder of Hadassah, in her small, simply furnished apartment. I told her of my day of interviewing and of my talk with Sir Harold MacMichael, of my confusion and of my anxiety to find the answer. I asked her if she thought it true that certain foreign powers were deliberately stirring up trouble between the Jew and the Arab to help sustain their own control.

She said: "With a sad heart I must tell you it is true."
Then she said to me, "Mr. Willkie, this problem has been
with me for many years. I cannot live comfortably in America while it is unsolved. There is no other appropriate place
in the world where the persecuted Jews of Europe can come.
And no matter how much we may wish it, that persecution
will not end in your lifetime or in mine. The Jews must have
a national homeland. I am an ardent Zionist, but I do not
believe that there is a necessary antagonism between the
hopes of the Jews and the rights of the Arabs. I am urging
my fellow Jews here in Jerusalem to do those simple things
that break down the prejudices, the differences between
people. I urge each of them to make friends with a few Arabs
to demonstrate by their way of life that we are not coming as
conquerors or destroyers, but as a part of the traditional life
of the country, for us a sentimental and religious homeland."

She told me of her belief in the possibilities of education,
and though she is an old lady, nearing eighty, her stories of
what had already been done on many of the Jewish farm
colonies and in Jewish industry under Zionist direction were
full of youth and vitality.

It is probably unrealistic to believe that such a complex
question as the Arab-Jewish one, founded in ancient
history and religion, and involved as it is with high international policy and politics, can be solved by good will
and simple honesty. But as I sat there that late afternoon
with the sun shining through the windows, lighting up that
intelligent, sensitive face, I, at least for the moment, won-

dered if she in her mature, selfless wisdom might not know more than all the ambitious politicians.

Coupled everywhere with the problem of education in the Middle East was that of medicine and public health. It is hard to travel anywhere in those lands without being uncomfortably conscious all the time of disease and pestilence, and it is hard to see a future for these peoples without a determined drive to improve their health and vitality.

As with education, a few natives and a few foreigners, especially Americans, have already shown what can be done. The malaria record of the United States Army detachments I saw in Egypt, Palestine, or Iran will be one of the exciting disclosures to be made after the war. Screened windows, double doors, careful inspection of servants, drainage of standing water, mosquito boots and mosquito netting have left a mark, I believe, on the imaginations of the peoples of the Middle East. After all, nobody likes malaria.

As public health is improved in these countries, it will have interesting consequences not to be found in any medical book. For health measures must be universal to be effective; disease is no respecter of persons. And as the ordinary man or woman shares in the advantages of a lower mortality rate and a more vigorous life, he is likely, unless I miss my guess, to grow fond of sharing.

Sleeping arrangements for visiting foreigners like our party were certainly not typical. In Jerusalem, as a guest of Sir Harold MacMichael, I found no mosquito bar on the bed but a long coiled snake of green punk on a table. I left mine strictly alone, but one of my companions lit his. He reported that it smoldered gently and agreeably through the night and gave him at least a sense of great security. In Bagdad great fans set in the ceiling whirled all night in the Bilat, the special guest palace where we were lodged. It had been constructed to house Prince Bertil of Sweden a few years ago. In Beirut, Syrian boys with fly swatters stalked carefully through the rooms of General Catroux's *Résidence des Pins* before we went to bed. You begin to understand the problem, though, not in watching these time-honored precautions for the privileged, but in examining a mosquito that seems as big as a dragonfly that has escaped all the traps set for him and is about to settle on your arm in the morning, while you uneasily remember the lectures and the warnings that have met you at every stop from New York to Bagdad.

The real public-health problem, of course, is poverty. Bilharziasis takes a frightening toll of lives in Egypt. It is a disease carried by snails which inhabit the Nile. Egyptians drink and bathe in the Nile and its tributary canals and suffer terribly from the devitalizing effects of the disease they catch from the water. The problem, however, is not only to eliminate the snails from the river but also to give the Egyptians a filtered water supply. And this costs money.

Trachoma blinds the eyes of little children in all hot countries, and we saw it on the streets of Cairo, of Jerusalem, of Bagdad. Even with medical care and prevention, however, we shall not eliminate it until people come to want a way of living that will make flies undesirable. That means adequate housing and refrigeration and screening.

Perhaps the most startling example we saw of bad health on a large scale was in Teheran, capital of Iran. The city's water supply runs through open gutters along the sides of the streets. People wash themselves and their clothes in it, pump it upstairs to their apartments, drink it, cook in it. The old proverb that water cleans itself after it turns over seven times may keep them quiescent, but it does not keep them from dysentery, cholera, malaria, and a dozen other water-carried diseases. Only one out of every five children born in Teheran lives to the age of six.

It is all very well to say, as some people did say to me in Cairo and Jerusalem, that "the natives don't want anything better than what they have." That is the argument that has been used everywhere for centuries against the advancement of the underprivileged, by those whose condition makes them satisfied with the *status quo.* Yet the history of civilization shows that the creation of economic conditions under which those who have little or nothing can improve their lot is not a dividing process but a multiplying one, by which the well-being of all society is advanced. Both education and public health in the Middle East, it seemed to me, depend on the achievement of a higher standard of living, and this in turn requires the introduction of modern technical and industrial methods of producing goods and services.

Undoubtedly such improvement in living standards will add to the markets of the world. For the Middle East is a vast, dry sponge, ready to soak up an infinite quantity and variety of goods and services. There is potential practical advantage, then, in encouraging better living standards among these peoples. But there is an even stronger and more urgent reason for facing this problem. For the present lack of equilibrium between these peoples and their world is a potential source of conflict, the possible origin of another war.

The facts are simple enough. If we had left the olive groves and the cotton fields and the oil wells of this region alone, we might not have had to worry about this equilibrium—at least not yet. But we have not left them alone. We have sent our ideas and our ideals, and our motion pictures and our radio programs, our engineers and our businessmen, and our pilots and our soldiers into the Middle East; and we cannot now escape the result.

In effect, this result has been to render obsolete and ineffective the old ways of life. A few miles from Cairo, I saw Egyptian boys not ten years old pumping water into irrigation ditches with pumps as primitive as the first wheel. Those little boys seemed docile enough, but they won't be for long. All of Egypt, in its curious position of "nonbelligerent alliance" with Great Britain, has shown as clearly as a nation can its fundamental indifference as to which side wins. This is not wholly Britain's fault, but it seems to me intimately linked with the way both the British and we ourselves have disregarded our obligations.

This problem, as it seems to me, of bringing the peoples of the Middle East into the twentieth century in technical and industrial terms is, in turn, intimately linked with the question of political self-government. Many Westerners whom I met and talked with in these countries told me the several reasons, valid in their minds, for the extremely primitive backwardness in which most Arabs live. These reasons ranged from the charge that Arabs actually prefer to die young to the statement that their religion prevents them from accumulating the capital with which to make the improvements they need in their way of life. To my mind, these reasons were mostly nonsense. Give any Arabs I saw a chance to feel that they were running their own show, and they would change the world they live in.

Freedom or self-government, talked about in the context of the Middle East, is too absolute a concept to be useful to an American. On the one hand, people who are against it point to the chaos and confusion which would result if all these peoples were suddenly left free to rule themselves. On the other hand, people who are for it paint too black a picture of Western influence in the Middle East, describing it as sheer imperialist exploitation and forgetting the very real gains which have come with French and British and American commercial expansion there.

The pragmatic, realistic truth lies in the middle. I found only very few Arabs or Jews or Egyptians or Iranians who wanted the West to get out lock, stock, and barrel, and at once. For the most part, they wanted an orderly, scheduled plan under which Britain and France would transfer to them a steadily increasing share of responsibility for their own government.

This seems to me a reasonable enough desire. In a country like Iraq, I saw that it can be satisfied. Iraq is one of the very few countries in the world which has passed through colonial status to that of mandated area and then become, technically, a free and sovereign state. I had some chance to see that its sovereignty was still circumscribed by British needs, but at least these were military needs, connected with the winning of the war.

I liked the men I met in Iraq. Prince Abdul Ilah, the Regent, gave me a state dinner under the stars in Bagdad that I shall remember all my life. He stood on a handsome carpet on a vast lawn to greet his guests. On other carpets near his stood the chiefs of his government. Some of them were in robes and turbans, including the Minister of Economics, curiously enough, and the President of the Senate, who is known locally to irreverent foreigners as "God," because of his handsome desert costume and his long beard. Others were in Western dress. Nearly every minister, I learned, had at some time held nearly every portfolio in the government.

"With a small deck of cards," an Iraqi friend told me, "you must shuffle them often."

A couple of nights later, another dinner was given, this time by Nuri as-Said Pasha, the Premier of Iraq. He is a small man, with a keen, inquisitive look on his face and one of the shrewdest minds I have ever met. He had been returned to power only in 1941 after the British had had to use troops to throw out Rashid Ali al Gailani, his predecessor, who had been bought by the Germans. Nuri was running Iraq as a nonbelligerent ally of Great Britain, with a keen desire to get into the fight, which he has since done. Sir Kinahan Cornwallis, British Minister at Bagdad and another of the tall, pipe-smoking, able, quiet, and very British Colonial Office empire-builders whom I met all through the Middle East, was undoubtedly a man to whom Nuri listened with, to put it mildly, respectful attention. But I suspected that Nuri was a realist, that he was not likely to bog down in any dispute over theoretically complete freedom from British control, and that he knew time was playing on his side in his struggle to build the first really modern and independent Arab state.

Nuri's dinner was an Arabian Nights picture of the Middle East. We had spent the day seeing Bagdad, its fantastic Shi'ah mosque sprouting gold minarets into the sky, its dusty adobe walls and houses, a bazaar where copper and silver craftsmen were making bowls and pitchers but the stores sold only machine-made trinkets from New York or Liverpool, one of the finest museums in the world filled with the Ur-Chaldee finds which date from the very beginning of our history, a café where we drank Arab coffee with crowds of people talking, reading papers, or playing backgammon around us. Even against this background, the dinner was fabulous.

After a few formal speeches, the dinner became a concert, and the concert became an exhibition of Arab dancing girls, and this in turn became a Western ball with English nurses and American soldiers up from Basra on the Persian Gulf and Iraqi officers dancing under an Arabian sky. No man could have sat through that evening and preserved any

notion that the East and the West will never meet, or that
Allah is determined to keep the Arabs a desert folk, ruled
by foreigners from across the seas.

The next day, flying from Bagdad to Teheran, I was thinking over the events of the night before. And I became aware
of certain sober undercurrents that had been beneath the
gaiety, the same undercurrents I had noticed before in talking with students, newspapermen, and soldiers throughout
the Middle East. It all added up to the conviction that these
newly awakened people will be followers of some extremist
leader in this generation if their new hunger for education
and opportunity for a release from old restrictive religious
and governmental practice is not met by their own rulers
and their foreign overlords. The veil, the fez, the sickness,
the filth, the lack of education and modern industrial development, the arbitrariness of government, all commingled
in their minds to represent a past imposed upon them by a
combination of forces within their own society and the self-
interest of foreign domination. Again and again I was asked:
does America intend to support a system by which our
politics are controlled by foreigners, however politely, our
lives dominated by foreigners, however indirectly, because
we happen to be strategic points on the military roads and
trade routes of the world? Or, they would say, to put it your
way: because we are strategic points which must be held to
prevent Axis or some other non-democratic domination of
the key military roads and trade routes of the world? Because
our canals, our seas, and our countries are necessary to the

34

control of the eastern Mediterranean and constitute the road to Asia?

I know this problem can be oversimplified in its statement and is not susceptible of easy answers. I know that the retention of points such as Suez, the eastern Mediterranean, and the roads through Asia Minor to the East obviously, if our Western democracy is not to be threatened by hostile forces, must be kept in both friendly and stabilized hands. Likewise, I know there is much historical and even present-day justification for the current "protective" colonial system. Pragmatically, however, in view of the ferment which is going on, it is a question whether that system can be maintained. Idealistically, we must face the fact that the system is completely antipathetic to all the principles for which we claim we fight. Furthermore, the more we preach those principles, the more we stimulate the ferment that endangers the system.

I know all this. But I am here reporting what is in the minds of Prime Ministers, Foreign Ministers, awakened intellectual groups to be found in every city of the Middle East, and even vaguely in the minds of uneducated masses. Somehow, with a new approach and a patient wisdom, the question must be answered or a new leader will arise with a fierce fanaticism who will coalesce these discontents. And the result will be of necessity either the complete withdrawal of outside powers with a complete loss of democratic influence or complete military occupation and control of the countries by those outside powers.

35

If we believe in the ends we proclaim and if we want the stirring new forces within the Middle East to work with us toward those ends, we must cease trying to perpetuate control by manipulation of native forces, by playing off one against the other for our own ends.

3

Turkey, a New Nation

THAT VAST and ancient portion of the globe which stretches from North Africa around the eastern end of the world's oldest sea and up to Bagdad on the road to China may well be the area in which our war will be won or lost. It is still a potential battleground; American tanks and planes are there with those of the British and the Fighting French and other United Nations. But it is more than a battleground; it is also a great social laboratory where ideas and loyalties are being tested by millions of people in the slow but inexorable process by which the war is also being fought, and won or lost, in the minds of men.

One's feeling that the Middle East is stirring and changing finds conviction in Turkey. For the Republic of Turkey has in one generation offered a possible prototype for what is happening to all the vast area that used to be the Ottoman Empire. And, in one form or another, the ideas which Turkey plants in the mind of an American today are reinforced by everything he sees all the way to the borders of Russia, China, and India.

Turkey is a new republic; it celebrated its nineteenth birthday last fall. It is weaker than some of its European neighbors; when I was there every Turk I spoke to was acutely conscious that his country might be attacked any day. Finally, it is far smaller than it once was—a sprawling empire become a neat, cohesive nation.

In spite of being young, and comparatively weak, and small, Turkey looked good to me. It looked good because it was quite clearly determined to defend its neutrality with every resource at its command. It looked good because it had set its face toward the modern world and was building, hard and fast. It looked good because I saw a great many tough and honest faces, some in uniform and some not, on people who quite obviously had a future to fight for. Finally, it looked good to me because I thought I saw, in Turkey, a nation which had found itself—a sign that the ideas of increasing health, education, freedom, and democracy are as valid in the oldest portions of the world as they are in the newest.

Ankara is not one of the world's large capitals. It is modern, with part of an ancient village left on a hill as if to remind the Turks how far they have already gone. From another hill, on which Ataturk, the father of the new republic, built his own home, you can walk down tree-shaded streets, with broad pavements, to the center of the city. The streets are full of cars; the people are well dressed and busy; the buildings are new and good-looking.

One day I drove out of Ankara, some forty miles into the country to the east. Outside the city's limits, you find yourself in ancient Anatolia. There are a hardness and strength about this countryside which help you understand why Ataturk so resolutely turned his back on Constantinople, the traditional Ottoman capital, now called Istanbul, and put his capital city here in the middle of the Anatolian plain.

For one thing, it is tough country to attack. A small army, well trained and well equipped, could hold this kind of countryside for a long time against invading, mechanized armies.

Shepherds graze their flocks in the hills. But even in the country, there was evidence of the reconstruction which Turkey has pushed so hard in the nineteen years since it became a republic. Men were building a new highway to the east; we drove by steam rollers and stone crushers at work on this road. There is a good deal of modern irrigation—the kind of irrigation which might someday transform large parts of Anatolia into prosperous farming country. The Turks are proud of their progress in public education, irrigation, and industrial developments and were anxious for us to see what they were doing.

In a village we visited, primarily to see a teachers' training school, they had built a house around the village spring. The house was of concrete and glass; it stood in the exact center of the village. On one side was water for drinking; on another there was provision for washing clothes; the children of the village had a stream to play in. As I stood and looked at this pleasant development, I saw veiled women sitting

39

motionless on the roof of a house in their traditional fashion. But I also saw boys and girls who were looking at the clean spring as I was—at something new and good and exciting.

I saw as much of Turkish industry as I could in a short stay. It is not impressive in size compared to the industries of the German nation which may attack it. But it is impressive in its quality and in the promise it holds for the future. I saw airfields and mechanized army equipment, and railroads, and the most advanced type of building construction. I saw all of these and more, and I convinced myself again that the industrial revolution is not the monopoly of any one nation or of any one race. The combustion engine has awakened millions of people in the Middle East— awakened and disturbed them. To these Turks, it has already brought new skills and new hungers. Now that they want the modern world, and have begun to learn how to handle its tools, it is going to be very hard to stop them.

Even more impressive than the industrial and economic reconstruction of Turkey, going on in the middle of the war, is the social and educational revolution which has taken place. To the visitor's eye in any country clothes furnish a surface indication of the attitude toward change. In Bagdad I had seen government officials, some wearing Western garb, others wearing the traditional robes of the Moslem. In China the President is reverenced for his compliance with the customs and the dress of old China, while Mme Chiang dresses in the Chinese manner but manages to give the effect of at least a glance at *Vogue*. In Turkey every official proudly and exclusively wears Western dress. The fez has been legally abolished as one of the symbols of the change. The few veiled women one encounters already seem an anachronism. Under the leadership of Ataturk and the determined, capable men who succeeded him, the Turks have literally and figuratively abolished the veils of the ancient East. They have stripped them from the faces of their people and the light that has replaced them is there, one feels, to stay.

And this revolution in age-old custom was brought about without badges or uniforms or mass hysteria. It was achieved without attacking any other country.

America has some reason for special pride in this. Roberts College, outside Istanbul, which I unfortunately could not visit, remains today what it has been for years—an unselfish experiment in the internationalism of education. Its graduates are now sitting behind some of the most important desks in Turkey. They are turning to good use the knowledge and ideas given them by American teachers who had no other purpose than to make the whole world richer by fighting against superstition and ignorance in one part of it.

But even Americans may have difficulty in understanding how deep this question of education cuts all over Asia. We take our schools and our books for granted. Our children are students without our wondering why or how.

In the Turkish countryside you see education for what it is to people who do not take it for granted. I stood in a plain little school, built by the children and their teachers, and listened to young Turkish boys sing their national anthem. I watched them learn their own national folk dances, embodying the gestures of the ancient crafts which once flourished in Anatolia. But they were being taught according to modern educational methods and they were studying scientific agriculture. It is my deep conviction that opening the books to people in this way is one of the decisive events of history. It is a turning in the road, and one from which there is no turning back.

Modern Turkey is a country which, in spite of its youth and the relative inexperience of its people with freedom and self-government, very definitely has something to fight for. You see this in the faces of people you talk with; you hear it in their speech. It is written large in their new cities, like Ankara, and in their old villages, like those I saw in the Turkish countryside.

But, very naturally, the Turks do not want to fight, knowing how terribly destructive to all their new accomplishment would be an invasion of the German legions. Turkey is a small country. Its sixteen million people have no ambitions outside their own frontiers, and they have no illusions about what they can do to swing the balance in this global war. So they have decided on a policy of armed neutrality. Last fall, they had more than a million of their men in the Turkish Army. They have developed a military machine which makes up in resoluteness and in training much of what it lacks in some branches of modern military equipment. I talked to the assistant chief of staff of the Turkish Army, and I saw his soldiers everywhere I went in the country, standing sentry duty, on maneuvers, in military schools. They impressed me as a very respectable problem for any aggressor nation that might want to use Turkey as a highway to conquest of the East.

Besides seeing Turkey's soldiers, I talked at very considerable length to the leaders of the country's government, the men who were watching Europe with the fearful anxiety of men who did not know when, or even if, they were going to be plunged into a war to save their country.

That is a terrible anxiety to live under. But not a single man in Turkey gave me the slightest hint that there would be anything other than bitter, determined, savage resistance to any threat which jeopardized their peace and safety.

I think this was more than a tale men might fix up to impress a visiting foreigner. I talked with Mr. Saracoglu, the talented and attractive man who is now Turkey's Prime Minister. I talked with Noumen Bey, the wise and distinguished diplomat who succeeded Mr. Saracoglu as Foreign Minister. I talked to many other members of the government, and to Turkish newspapermen, and to soldiers and to peasants and to workingmen. And the story each of these men told me was the same: "We don't want a war or any part of it. But the first soldier who crosses our frontier will be shot, and before we have stopped shooting in our hills and along our roads and in our forests, there will be a lot of dead foreigners."

They always spoke of "foreigners," and they always insisted that their determination to fight was directed against any country which might attack them, from any direction. But it was clear without their saying it that their immediate fears were riveted in one direction. Today they do not fear us, or our English allies who are also Turkey's allies, or the hard-pressed Russians, although they are troubled about Russia's ultimate designs. Their immediate anxiety lies in the West, in the top-heavy power which has been built up in Europe in the last few years and which threatens to spill over into Asia, across their territory. They look with anxiety and with fear, because they do not want to fight, but not with panic and not with any notion of appeasement. Germany has twice attempted a major "peace offensive" in their capital. And it has twice failed.

They would like to deal with us. They are prepared to trade goods. They produce, in Turkey, nearly one-quarter of the world's supply of chrome. Their tobacco and their cotton are badly needed by other countries. With these assets, the Turks can buttress their neutrality, for a time, at any rate. They need foodstuffs—wheat especially—and they need manufactures and machinery, as I was at pains to discover. And I have been greatly pleased that since my return we have been sending them increasingly large quantities of foodstuffs and other materials. For we are today the only country which can adequately supply them. I deeply believe that it is to our interest to do so, as far as we are able, to prevent Turkish resources from going to our enemies, and to preserve the neutrality of a country which wants to be our friend.

And of that there can be no doubt. Nearly a decade of the heavy pounding of Dr. Goebbels and his Nazi propaganda machine has not changed the slower but deeper trend of the awakening people of Turkey toward closer relations with

44

the world's great democracies. The Turks are our friends. They both like and admire us. They do not fear us, nor do they envy us.

Their neutrality, however, is honestly administered. They refused, for example, to allow me to come to their country in the United States Army plane which took me around the world, and I had to change at Cairo into a Pan-American Airways plane to fly up the eastern coast of the Mediterranean and over the bleak and bumpy Taurus Mountains to Ankara. At the airfield where we landed we saw the three carefully guarded Liberator bombers which the Turks had interned after American fliers had been forced down on their return from raids on the oil fields at Ploeşti, in Rumania.

But underneath this neutral correctness, there was a cordiality no one could mistake. When the Axis radio during my visit complained of my presence in Turkey, I told the newspapermen that the answer was simple: "Invite Hitler to send to Turkey, as a representative of Germany, his opposition candidate." The remark, I found afterward, caused much quiet amusement among Turkish government officials.

Interestingly enough, although nationalism in Turkey has been the slogan under which so much has been accomplished, Turkey and its officials have more receptiveness to the necessity of international co-operation beyond and outside its own immediate needs than any other country I visited. This was emphasized to me in all the long and frank talks I had with the Prime Minister, the Foreign Minister, and the leading publishers.

Of course, as in all capitals, one sees amusing manifestations of an international society. One night, Noumen Bey, the Foreign Minister, gave a dinner outside of Ankara. It was at the country house of Ataturk, a model farm and dairy which he started outside the city limits. At least, they told me it was a model farm; all I saw was a handsome modern palace on a hill with terraced flower gardens stepping down toward the lights of Ankara in the distance.

In one room of this house, used now by the Foreign Minister for official entertainments, there was a telephone that had been used by Ataturk, made of solid gold. In another room was an old-fashioned Turkish machine for making "shish-kebab"; a chef turned slowly an enormous cylinder of mutton over an open charcoal fire, slicing its cooked surface into bowls of rice.

In the main ballroom stood Noumen Bey, our host. He is one of the most accomplished foreign diplomats of this generation, on his record, and he looks the part. His health is not good, but his pallor and a general frailty only emphasize the courtly skill with which he seems to be watching Europe and the world. I found his mind, like his appearance, a little sad, a little cynical, very strong, and very subtle.

Around him danced or drank or talked the diplomats of all the countries on our side. Axis-inspired newspapermen had come to the press conference I held in Ankara, but the Axis diplomats in Turkey do not mix at parties with those of the United Nations. There was still variety enough. The

Soviet Ambassador was in Moscow on a trip, but his chargé d'affaires was at the party, very correct in evening clothes—I had none—but with a grim, unlaughing manner. A tall English lady in marabou feathers seemed in striking contrast. Later I learned her husband had fought in Crete. The representatives of Greece and Yugoslavia came up to me with their arms around each other's shoulders to tell me their plans for the confederation of Europe. Another diplomat, whose name I never learned, told me with excitement but with bewildering inaccuracy that he had heard that an American boxer named Conn had just knocked out Joe Louis. The magnificent-looking Ambassador of Afghanistan complained to me that he had taken his post at Ankara chiefly for the hunting and now found that Turkey's preparedness measures barred him from his favorite sport.

In all this confusion, which mirrored well enough the world we live in, the figure of my host, Noumen Bey, grew in stature. Like his predecessor in the Foreign Ministry and present chief, Saracoglu, he drew his strength from no aristocracy of birth or of doctrine. He had fought hard through a long life, first by the side of Ataturk and the Turkish people, and now with the Turkish people alone. I watched him that night at his own party, at which we drank English whisky and ate Russian caviar and danced to American music in the curious internationalism of the diplomatic world, and I was more than ever convinced that the Turkish people have put their bets on a different world emerging from this war.

Like the redheaded, blue-eyed children who surprised me

47

every time I saw them in Turkey, or the hard, iron-faced soldiers on the streets, or the schoolteachers who had learned their soft, pleasant English at Roberts College, Noumen Bey seemed to me to personify a vast leaven which is now working deep in the lives of something more than half the human race. He was the product of an ancient people, and a proud tradition, but he was living through, in his own generation, one of the most profound changes ever experienced by any people.

In the last war, Turkey was on the German side. The Ottoman Empire, out of the ruins of which this new republic grew, was popular nowhere in the world. Even the word "Turk" was an evil word.

The change has been so quick that many of us have missed it. For something less than two decades, the phenomenal struggle of Ataturk and his friends, like Noumen Bey and Saracoglu, has channeled the energies and ambitions of their people into new ways of living.

Like the Arabs of the Middle East, like the peoples who live around the borders of China or on the islands of the southwest Pacific, like the Indians, they had no experience with self-government until a generation ago. They had almost no education, wretched standards of public health and sanitation, and a long history of exploitation and poverty and misery. In a few brief years they have completely transformed their habits of life, their ancient customs, and their ways of thinking.

A woman I came to know in Turkey brought these changes home to me in a peculiarly real fashion. She was pure Turk, an attractive, middle-aged woman who spoke English well and whose conversation was that of any intelligent woman today. She was a resident of Istanbul but was in Ankara arguing a series of cases before the Turkish Supreme Court. For she is a lawyer, one of Turkey's most distinguished lawyers, with a large practice. The fact that she was a woman and a lawyer excited no particular comment that I could see. In fact, I met several other young women who were studying law, including daughters of government officials.

And this was in Turkey. I could not help thinking of my boyhood days when, only forty years ago, my mother's active practice of the law and interest in public affairs were considered an unusual—almost a peculiar—thing in central Indiana.

4

Our Ally, Russia

O N THURSDAY, September 18, I flew into the Soviet
Union over the Caspian Sea, across the salt, red mud
flats at the delta of the Ural River, and up to the Volga
River at Kuibishev. I left Russia ten days later, flying down
the Ili River along the old silk route to China from Tashkent in central Asia. Later, on the way home from China,
our plane again made three landings in Russia, in Siberia.

I was in Russia a total of only two weeks. I had never
been there before. I do not speak a word of Russian, but I
had Americans with me to act as interpreters. I had read a
great deal about the Soviet Union, but nothing I had read
had ever given me a very clear picture of what was going
on in that vast country. Finally, I suspected before I went
to Russia, and became more and more certain as I stayed
there, that the country is so vast and the change it has gone
through so complicated that only a lifetime of study and a
shelfful of books could begin to tell the whole truth about
the Soviet Union.

It is true, and worth reporting, that the Soviet government gave me every chance to find out what I wanted to learn. It permitted me to examine in my own way its industrial and war plants, its collective farms, its schools, its libraries, its hospitals, its war front. I came and went as freely as though I had been making a similar trip through the United States, and I asked questions—unexpected questions of unexpected people—without limit or interference, and always in the presence of an American who understood and spoke Russian.

A visitor for the first time to Russia inevitably reflects now and then upon the past. One late afternoon in Kuibishev I found myself thinking of pre-revolutionary times. I walked alone to the edge of the steep bank on the western side of the Volga and sat on a park bench looking down at the river. The government had given us a Red Army rest home right at the river's edge. There was a biting cold already in the air, but the leaves were still on the trees. Along the bank stretched small, unpainted *dachas*—the country bungalows of which Russians are so fond—and pine trees, and there was an air of deep quiet and strength, like the great river below. Beyond the pine trees was wheat land rolling down the river to Stalingrad, where Russian soldiers were holding a mass of rubble against Nazi tanks and planes.

At the river's edge, below me, a boat had finished unloading its cargo of birch logs. The logs were stacked in a pile that must have covered several acres. With the Don

Basin lost, with war industries getting every lump of coal available, this was the only fuel Russian cities would have to burn in the cold winter to come. A shepherd led a flock of sheep along the shore. In the middle of the river a tanker, loaded full, was moving slowly upstream. A young Russian soldier walked along the path behind the sheep, kicking pebbles into the river with his foot. When he took off his hat, the wind ruffled his hair to make him look even younger, and it was only then that I noticed his hat had the insignia of the NKVD, or secret police.

I thought of the pre-1917 shipbuilder who had built the resthouse behind me as a summer home. I had been told that he had been a power in the land, a tight-fisted ship-owner and grain merchant who had prospered in the commerce of the Volga when the town had been called Samara and been liquidated when it was called Kuibishev, for the Samaran revolutionist who devised the first Five-Year Plan. The house had stayed, a little less shabby than its neighbors, because the Red Army had found it useful.

I could see, it seemed to me, the entire generation of men and women who had been destroyed, the families that had been scattered, the loyalties that had been broken, the thousands who had died from war and assassination and starvation, in the name of the revolution.

The true story of that period will probably never be told in detail. For except for those who escaped to other lands, and they were relatively few, practically the whole upper and middle classes of Russia have been completely exterminated. And Russians today find the story a heroic achievement.

I had not realized before coming to Russia to what extent that is true. For I had not sufficiently taken into account, in appraising modern Russia, that it is ruled by and composed almost entirely of people whose parents had no property, no education, and only a folk heritage. That there is hardly a resident of Russia today whose lot is not as good as or better than his parents' lot was prior to the revolution. The Russian individual, like all individuals, naturally finds some good in a system that has improved his own lot, and has a tendency to forget the ruthless means by which it has been brought about. This may be difficult for an American to believe or like. But it was plainly the explanation among all sorts of people, everywhere, and it was clearly expressed during a stimulating evening I spent in Moscow when I was trying to put a group of intelligent modern Russians on the spot to defend their system.

But I had not gone to Russia to remember the past. Besides my concrete assignments for the President, I had gone determined to find an answer for myself to the actual problems posed for our generation of Americans by the simple fact that the Soviet Union, whether we like it or not, exists.

Some of these answers I believe I found, at least to my own satisfaction. I can sum up the three most important in a few sentences.

First, Russia is an effective society. It works. It has survival value. The record of Soviet resistance to Hitler has been proof enough of this to most of us, but I must admit in all frankness that I was not prepared to believe before I went to Russia what I now know about its strength as a going organization of men and women.

Second, Russia is our ally in this war. The Russians, more sorely tested by Hitler's might even than the British, have met the test magnificently. Their hatred of Fascism and the Nazi system is real and deep and bitter. And this hatred makes them determined to eliminate Hitler and exterminate the Nazi blight from Europe and the world.

Third, we must work with Russia after the war. At least it seems to me that there can be no continued peace unless we learn to do so.

Those conclusions were reinforced by what I saw and heard in various parts of the Soviet Union. I saw one portion of the Russian front, close enough to know something at first hand of what the Red Army has done. I saw a good many of the factories behind the front, where the Soviet workers have fooled too many of our experts by keeping up a steady flow of supplies to the fighting men. And I saw collective farms. Behind the factories and the farms, I saw and talked with the Soviet newspapermen and writers who have given all Russians the strangely exalted feeling of being in a crusade. Behind the journalists, I saw the Kremlin, having talked twice at great length with Mr. Stalin, and observed something of how power is really exercised under the dictatorship of the proletariat. Finally, behind all these, I saw the Russian people from one end of Russia to the other, and if my sampling of the 200,000,000 was absurdly small, it had the advantage of being chosen entirely by chance.

One of the most enlightening experiences I had was a trip to the fighting front at Rzhev. To get to Rzhev from Moscow, you must drive up the Leningrad highway running to Kalinin, which used to be called Tver, then westward to Klin and on a little farther to a small country town called Staritsa. We had started out in comfortable cars, riding all night. At dawn, at Staritsa, we changed to American-made jeeps. With me were General Philip Faymonville, Major General Follet Bradley, Colonel Joseph A. Michela, the American Military Attaché in Russia, as well as four members of my party and our Russian guides.

The jeep is a great invention, and as an American I am proud of it. After fourteen hours in one, however, I had acquired an intimacy with its structure, its angles and corners, and its bucking gait that dulled some of my feeling of pride in its American origin. For endless hours, over what seemed endless miles, we bumped and bounced on roads so rough and muddy and rutted and corduroyed that for the first time I really understood the stories my father used to tell me of conditions in pioneer Indiana.

At last we came to the headquarters, north of Rzhev, of Lieutenant General Dmitri D. Lelyushenko, a man so colorful and engaging that among all the personalities I have met he stands out vividly. He was only thirty-eight years old, but a lieutenant general in charge of sixteen divisions of fighting men at one of the most important fighting fronts in the world.

He is a man of medium height, powerfully built, a born horseman with bowed legs betraying his Cossack origin, ruddy, vital, alert, full of animal spirits. He took us to his underground headquarters. He explained his battle maps, the placement of his troops, his plan of attack, the momentary changes in the battle then raging ahead of and around us.

He was then beginning the move to bypass Rzhev and cut the railroad to Vyazma which was accomplished some weeks after we had returned to the United States, preliminary to the dramatic lifting of the siege of Leningrad. From his headquarters in a grove of fir trees on a hill, we could see and hear the artillery beyond the town about eight miles from us.

I was struck by the eagerness of his staff. The general had only to begin a sentence and two or three adjutants were standing at attention, waiting for his order. I was also struck by the number of girls and women in uniform. Besides communications, sanitary and transport work, they stood guard at the observation posts we saw in trees around the general's headquarters and at the underground dugouts where the officers did their work.

From headquarters we drove on, nearer to the battle, and inspected a German strong point which had recently been captured by the Russians. What had once been a small village, on the brow of a little hill, was a mass of wreckage, mud, hamlets, and corpses which had not yet been buried. In the bottom of a trench, I saw a can, unopened but half buried in the mud, marked LUNCHEON HAM in English, and I wondered on which other front in this global war the Germans had picked it up.

The general told me his troops had just taken some German prisoners and asked me if I would like to see them. I said I would and that I would like to talk to them too. The general replied, "I have been instructed to let you do whatever you wish."

I took one look at his freshly captured prisoners, fourteen of them standing forlornly in a line. I looked again, more closely. Then I said to myself: Are these thinly dressed, emaciated, consumptive-looking men the same terrifying Huns, the unbeatable soldiers about whom I have read so many tales?

Through interpreters I began to talk to them. I asked them where they lived in Germany, their ages, whether they got letters from home, how their families were getting along without them, and a multitude of other simple, kindly questions. With the answers, the last vestige of a German military front disappeared. These soldiers became miserable, homesick boys and men. Some were almost forty and some were only seventeen.

I turned to the general and told him what I was thinking.

"That's right, Mr. Willkie," he answered, "but don't be misled. The German equipment is still superb, and the German officers are proficient and professional. German army organization is unmatched. Even with such men as you see here, the German Army is still the greatest fighting military organization in the world. But if your nation will send us the equipment we need, the Red Army will outfight them on every front from the Caucasus to the North

Pole. For our men are better, and they are fighting for their homeland."

I think his men were better, and it was clear all through that day and the day following that they were fighting for their homeland. A few miles behind the front, we saw Russian peasants with their belongings piled high on farm wagons, a cow hitched behind each wagon, plodding slowly along the roads. The striking thing was that they were moving not away from the front, but toward it, surging back with a kind of elemental strength to the land which the Red Army had won back from the enemy. The villages they found were nothing but gaunt chimneys against the sky, but it was time for fall plowing, so back they went.

A drizzling, cold rain—foretaste of what the Germans were to face a month or two later—delayed our departure, and the general invited us to supper with him. About forty of us, Soviet officers and soldiers and their visitors, managed to squeeze into one tent. We ate cold boiled bacon and rye bread, tomatoes and cucumbers and pickles, and toasted each other in vodka.

Unthinkingly, during supper, I asked the interpreter to ask the general just how large a section of Russia's two-thousand-mile front he was defending. The general looked at me as if offended, and the interpreter repeated after him, slowly, "Sir, I am not defending. I am attacking."

After my visit to the Rzhev front, I realized more clearly than ever before that in Russia the phrase "This is a people's war" has real meaning. It is the Russian people in the fullest sense who are resolved to destroy Hitlerism. What they have been through and what they face in the months ahead cannot fail to stir any American. Stalin had given me certain facts about Russia's great sacrifices and desperate needs before I went to the front and I had seen ample evidence of both with my own eyes.

Already five million Russians had been killed, wounded, or were missing. The great fertile farm lands of southwestern Russia were largely in Nazi hands. Their products were feeding the enemy and their men and women were forced to be his slaves. Thousands of Russia's villages had been destroyed and their people were homeless. Her transportation system was overloaded; her factories, producing to the very limit, required the full output of her remaining oil fields and coal mines.

Food in Russia was scarce—perhaps worse than scarce. There would be little fuel in Russian homes in the approaching winter. Even when I was in Moscow women and children were gathering wood from fifty miles around to make a little warmth against the coming cold. Clothing, except for the army and essential war workers, was nearly gone. Many vital medical supplies just did not exist.

This was the picture I got of wartime Russia. Yet no Russian talked of quitting. They all knew what had happened in the Nazi-occupied countries. The Russian people —not just their leaders—the Russian people, I was convinced, had chosen victory or death. They talked only of victory.

I spent one entire day looking at a Soviet aviation plant. I saw other factories in Russia, candy factories, munition factories, foundries, canneries, and power plants. But this aviation plant, now located outside of Moscow, remains most vivid in my memory.

It was a big place. My guess would be that some 30,000 workers were running three shifts and that they were making a very presentable number of airplanes every day. The plane produced was the now-famous Stormovik, a single-engined, heavily armored fighting model which has been developed by the Russians as one of the really novel weapons of the war. It has a low ceiling, and climbs slowly, so that it actually needs a fighter escort. But used as an anti-tank weapon, traveling low and at high speed and carrying heavy fire power, it has been one of the Red Army's most powerful weapons.

American aviation experts were with me on this inspection, and they confirmed my impression that the planes we saw wheeled from the end of the assembly line and tested on an airfield next to the factory were good planes. And, peculiarly enough, they pronounced the armored protection for the pilots the best of any they knew on any plane anywhere in the world. I am no aviation expert, but I have inspected a good many factories in my life. I kept my eyes open, and I think my report is fair.

Parts of the manufacturing process were crudely organized. The wings of the Stormovik are made of plywood, compressed under steam pressure, and then covered with canvas. The woodworking shops seemed to me to rely too much on hand labor, and their product showed it. Also, some of the electrical and plating shops were on the primitive side.

With these exceptions, the plant would compare favorably in output and efficiency with any I have ever seen. I walked through shop after shop of lathes and punching presses. I saw machine tools assembled from all over the world, their trade-names showing they came from Chemnitz, from Skoda, from Sheffield, from Cincinnati, from Sverdlovsk, from Antwerp. They were being efficiently used.

More than thirty-five per cent of the labor in the plant was done by women. Among the workers we saw boys not more than ten years old, all dressed in blue blouses and looking like apprentice students, even though the officials of the factory pulled no punches in admitting that the children work, in many of the shops, the full sixty-six-hour week worked by the adults. Many of the boys were doing skilled jobs on lathes, and seemed to be doing them extremely well.

On the whole, the plant seemed to us Americans to be overstaffed. There were more workers than would be found in a comparable American factory. But hanging over every third or fourth machine was a special sign, indicating that its worker was a "Stakhanovite," pledged to overfulfill his or her norm of production. The Stakhanovites, strange as it may seem to us, are actually pieceworkers, paid at a progressively increasing rate on a speed-up system which is like an accelerated Bedeaux system. The Russian industrial system is a strange paradox to an American. The method of employing and paying labor would satisfy our most unso-cial industrialist. And the way capital is treated would, I believe, completely satisfy a Norman Thomas. The walls of the factory carried fresh and obviously honored lists of those workers and those shops which were leading in what was apparently a ceaseless competition for more and better output. A fair conclusion would be that this extra incentive, which was apparent in the conversation of any worker we stopped to talk to at random, made up for a large part, but not all, of the handicap of relative lack of skill.

The productivity of each individual worker was lower than in the United States. Russian officials admitted this to me freely. Until they can change this by education and training, they explained, they must offset it by putting great emphasis on patriotic drives for output and by recruiting all the labor power, even that of children and old women, that they can find. Meanwhile, and there was nothing done with mirrors here, we could see the planes leaving the cavernous doors of the final assembly unit, testing their machine guns and cannon on a target range, and then taking to the air over our heads.

The director of the plant, a grave-faced man in his late thirties, named Tretyakov, took us to lunch in his office. We walked through long corridors, lit only by dim blue electric lights, to a simple room, entirely blacked out, where he worked. On a conference table were sandwiches, hot tea, cakes, the usual caviar, and the ubiquitous bottles of vodka. In a corner stood two flags, both awarded to the plant by the Kremlin for its successful fulfillment of its plan.

Tretyakov offered to answer my questions. He sat at the head of the table. A small, thin silver star was the only insignia on his dark business suit. I later learned that he was one of only seven Soviet civilians who have been given this star, emblem of the title of "Hero of the Soviet Union."

After an hour of detailed cross-examination, it was clear to me that he would have been an outstanding leader in any society I have ever known. He spoke quietly, gravely, with a full sense of the national and international urgency of his work, with an obviously detailed knowledge of what went on in every corner of his enormous plant. A few questions I put to him, such as the number of planes produced daily, the exact number of workers, the exact top speed of the Stormovik, he turned aside politely but firmly. When I tried to get the same information by more subtle approaches, his eyes twinkled, but he was not fooled into betraying any military secrets, any more than a responsible factory manager in England or America would be.

This plant, he told us, had been picked up bodily from its foundations in Moscow in October, 1941, when the sound of Nazi cannonading could be heard in the Soviet capital. It had been moved more than a thousand miles over a transport system already loaded down with the requirements of a nation in arms. It had been set up again, many of its original workers tending their own machines throughout the transfer, and by December, two months later, it was producing planes at its new location.

During that first winter of 1941-42, he told me, there was no heating in the plant. Workers built bonfires in the shops

to keep their machines from freezing. There was no housing ready for the workers, and many of them slept next to
their tools. By the fall of 1942, things were better organized.
Factory restaurants, for example, which I had seen, apparently served simple but adequate and nourishing food to
the workers. But I knew that in the same town the only
food that could be bought in the markets was black bread
and potatoes, and at exorbitant prices.

As the luncheon broke up, I began to question a short,
wiry young fellow whom the director had introduced to me
as the superintendent of production, his bright young man.
He was dressed in worker's clothes, with the mechanic's cap
which is almost the badge of an industrial worker in Russia.
He was a trained engineer, with an alert, almost jaunty manner, energetic, intelligent, and with a thorough knowledge
of his job; the kind of young man that in American industrial life would make rapid advancement, acquire a compe-
tence, and become a leader among his fellows. In fact, he
reminded me so much of the promising American industrial
type that I decided to try to find out from him what were the
urges and the lures under the Communist system that caused
him to educate himself beyond his fellows, to work the extra
hours necessary to become superintendent over 30,000 men,
and to acquire the knowledge that was clearly leading him
toward the top.

He said he'd be glad to answer my questions. He told me
that he was thirty-two years old, married, and the father of
two children. He lived in a comfortable house much better
than the average, and in peacetime had an automobile.

"How does your pay as superintendent of this factory compare with the pay of the average skilled worker in the plant?" I asked him.

He thought for a moment: "It's about ten times as much."

That would be on the same ratio twenty-five or thirty thousand dollars a year in America, and actually was about what a man of similar responsibility in America would receive. So I said to him, "I thought Communism meant equality of reward."

Equality, he told me, was not part of the present Soviet conception of socialism. "From each according to his capacities, to each according to his *work*," was the slogan of Stalinist socialism, he explained, and only when they had achieved the Communist phase of their development would the slogan be changed to "From each according to his capacities, to each according to his *needs*." Even then, he added, complete equality would not be necessary or desirable.

"With such an income normally you are able to save, to put aside something, aren't you?" I went on.

He laughed and said, "Yes, if my wife doesn't spend too much."

"What do you do with your savings? How do you invest them?"

"With my first savings, we bought ourselves a nice house," he told me.

"And then?"

"Then we bought a place in the country, where the family

could go for vacation and I could go for a rest, or to fish and hunt when I could get away from the factory."

"And now that you have these things all paid for, what do you do with your extra money?"

"Oh, I keep it in cash, or put it in government bonds."

Soviet government bonds are non-interest-bearing, and remembering the first money I accumulated and the thought I gave to getting as much income from it as possible, I asked him, just to see what his answer would be, "Why don't you invest it in something that will give you a good return?"

He looked at me in surprise and, I thought, even with a slight air of superiority. "You mean, Mr. Willkie, to get return on capital? That isn't possible in Russia, and anyhow I don't believe in it."

I tried to get him to tell me why, and for ten minutes I found myself listening to Marxist and Leninist theories which I finally interrupted with the question:

"Well, what does cause you to work so hard?"

He answered, sweeping his arm about him as he spoke, "I run this factory. Someday I'll be the director. Do you see these badges?" pointing to a string of decorations pinned on his blouse. "Those were given to me by the party and the government because I was good." He spoke with frank cockiness. "Someday, if I'm good enough, the party will give me something to do with running the government."

"But who will take care of you when you are an old man?"

"I'll have some cash put aside, and if I don't have enough, the government will provide for me."

66

"Don't you ever have a desire to own a plant of your own?" I asked.

To which he replied with another deluge of Marxian economic and social philosophy with which he was as familiar as with the working of his plant.

"Well, how about your family?" I persisted. "Don't you want your children to have a better start than you had? Don't you want to protect your wife in case you go before she does?"

He said impatiently, "That's mere capitalistic talk, Mr. Willkie. I started as a worker. My children will have as good a start as I had. My wife works now, and as long as she's well she'll continue to work. When she's unable to do so, the state will take care of her."

"Well," I said, "what happens to you if you don't make good in this job?"

And he said with a grim smile, "I'll be liquidated." I knew that might mean anything from demotion to death itself. But he obviously thought that there was little danger that *he* would not make good.

I then tried to tackle him from another angle.

"Suppose—in ordinary times, not wartime—suppose you don't like your director here. Can you leave and get a job in some other factory?"

"Most workers could, but as a party member, I must stay where the party thinks I can do the most good."

"But suppose you should prefer to work at a different kind of job. Can you change your job?"

"That's for those in authority to say."

"I understand that you are in complete accord with the economic and political theories of the state. But if you happened to hold different ideas, could you express them and fight for them?"

It took me ten minutes of hot colloquy to get him even to consider such a supposition, and then his answer was only a shrug of the shoulders. It was my turn to be impatient and I said, somewhat sharply, "Then actually you've got no freedom."

He drew himself up almost belligerently and said, "Mr. Willkie, you don't understand. I've had more freedom than my father and grandfather ever had. They were peasants. They were never allowed to learn to read or write. They were slaves to the soil. When they sickened, there were no doctors or hospitals for them. I am the first man in the long chain of my ancestors who has had the opportunity to educate himself, to advance himself—to amount to anything. And that for me is freedom. It may not seem freedom to you, but, remember, we are in the developing stage of our system. Someday we'll have political freedom, too."

I pressed him: "How can you ever have political freedom and economic freedom where the state owns everything?"

He poured out his theories in a seemingly endless rush. But he had no answers beyond the Marxian ones in which he was so well grounded, and to that basic question, Marxism gives no answer.

As I turned to go, I overheard Major Kight, our amazingly skillful and intelligent pilot, say to Joe Barnes, "Listen, don't let's get away before you explain to that fellow that Mr. Willkie was just trying to get him to talk. Sure, we in America like what money will buy and want to get ahead a bit, but it's not only money that makes us work. This insignia on my shoulder brought me a big raise in pay when I got it. But at the same time I got this piece of ribbon here," pointing to the ribbon of the Distinguished Flying Cross, "and that didn't bring me a cent. You tell him that I'd give the rank and the pay raise back for nothing, but I wouldn't give away the ribbon for a million dollars."

Russia's farms, just as much as its factories, have been mobilized for total war, and their capacity to support a fighting nation has been one of Hitler's most profound miscalculations and one of the world's surprises.

Day after day we flew over these farms, all the way from the front itself, at Rzhev, to the farthest limits of cultivation in Central Asia and Siberia. For Russia's farming lands stretch nearly six thousand miles behind the front. Only from the air, I suspect, can one get any sense of the immensity of this farming land, or of its infinite variety. Parts of it, with grain crops running to the horizon, made our pilot, Major Kight, homesick for his native state of Texas. Other parts, like the irrigated valley near Tashkent, look like southern California.

On the Volga near Kuibishev, I had a chance to see some of these farms at closer range. We went up the river in a neat, modern river boat. Through the trees along the banks could be seen the rooftops of stately homes, once the country estates of the wealthy from as far away as Moscow and

St. Petersburg, now rest homes and sanitariums for workers. They reminded me of the great houses one sees from a Hudson River boat. But the Volga is more tricky than the Hudson—as I found for myself when our pilot once let me try his wheel. Suddenly we were among cross currents that rapidly sent us shoreward, much to the delight of the laughing Volga boatmen. Down the river floated great rafts of logs bound for lumber mills, with little huts built on them and cattle and chickens for the families who float slowly on these rafts all summer from the forests of north Russia to the cities of the south.

I had been told in Kuibishev of plans to dam a great bend in the Volga River for the production of electric power; and on this trip we went over the part of the Volga concerned in the proposed development. I am not one to be easily surprised by vast governmental power developments, but when it became clear that this one development, if completed, would produce twice as much power as all the TVA, the Grand Coulee, and the Bonneville developments combined, I began to realize that the Russians dream and plan on a scale to fit their vast forests and plains.

We left the Volga bend to drive inland to a collective farm which had formerly been a hunting estate of a member of the lesser nobility. It had some 8000 acres, with fifty-five families living on it, a ratio of about 140 acres per family, which is about the size of the average farm in Rush County, Indiana.

The soil was good—a dark, rich loam—but the rainfall was slight, only some thirteen inches per year. In Indiana we have about forty. Crops were cultivated without benefit of fertilizer, and cultivation was almost exclusively mechanical. Largely wheat and rye and other small grains were grown. The season's average yield per acre of wheat was fifteen and one-half bushels; of rye a little less, which I thought pretty good under the circumstances. To get this acreage yield, incidentally, required some concentrated figuring on the part of Mike Cowles and myself, involving the transposition of hectares to acres, and poods to bushels. We gave up trying to arrive at a comparable price per bushel in American money. For all quotations were given us in rubles, and we found that the value of the ruble is subject to rapid fluctuation and varies in different markets. We could, however, judge the quality of the grain, and it seemed to us good.

Each of the fifty-five families on the farm was allowed to own one cow; the scraggly herd, consisting of every known mixture as to breed, grazed together on a common near a cluster of small houses in which the families lived. But the collectivist farm itself owned 800 head of cattle, 250 of them cows, of excellent stock and all well cared for. The cattle barns were of brick and large; the floors were concrete and the stanchions modern. The calves were almost tenderly watched over, in clean neat stalls, and women who were in charge of the barns explained to me their methods of improving the stock by care and breeding. The methods were scientific and modern.

I saw only one able-bodied man on the farm; he was the manager. Most of the workers were women or children, with a few old men. For the farms of Russia have been the enormous reservoir from which the Red Army has been recruited, and the wives and children of Red Army soldiers are today feeding the country.

The manager was the czar of the farm. He was a man of scientific agricultural training, alert and assured. He planned the crops and directed the work. Every man, woman, and child on the place was under his authority.

He, in turn, was responsible for the success of the project and for the production of the farm's quota in the war economy. He would rise in power and in status if he succeeded; his punishment would be severe if he failed.

I was curious about the economy of one of these farms and asked many questions. A careful record of how much each member works is kept, I was told, in the farm office. The unit is a "workday," but special skills are recognized, so that a tractor-driver, for example, who plows a certain number of acres in a day is credited with two "workdays." The binding of a certain number of sheaves, or the tending of a certain number of cows, similarly constitutes an extra "workday."

This farm, like most of the collective farms of Russia, rented its tractors and mechanical equipment from government-owned machine stations, and payment was made from the farm's harvest, not in rubles but in kind. Then the farm had to pay taxes, which constitute almost a rental payment to the government, also in kind. The balance of each harvest was distributed to the members of the farm on the basis of how many "workdays" each had accumulated on the records.

What each member received in this final distribution of the harvest could be traded for manufactured goods at a small store on the farm property, or it could be sold. The government, however, has put steadily increasing pressure on the collective farmers to sell their crops directly to the government, though in theory they remain free to sell anywhere they wish after they have paid in kind for the machines they have used and their taxes. It seemed to me that most of the farmers I talked to had plenty of cash, with no way to spend it. For goods in the stores were scarce and steadily decreasing as a result of the almost complete absorption of all factories by the war and the needs of the Red Army.

We went to the home of the farm manager for lunch. He was a man of thirty-seven, married, with two children. He lived in a small stone house, simple, and in atmosphere not very different from a prosperous farmhouse in the United States. It was a hearty hospitality, with much laughing good humor. The food was abundant, simple but good, and the wife of the manager, who had cooked the meal, urged me to eat as I have been urged many times in Indiana farm houses: "Mr. Willkie, do have some more. You've hardly eaten a thing." And then, of course, there was the ever-present vodka. Water was nowhere in sight.

I pressed the manager and his wife, and talked with some of the workers on the farm, trying to find out how it was that they were free of the consuming urge of every farmer

I ever knew to own his own bit of land. To some of them it even seemed strange that I inquired. But the manager explained that he and the rest were less than a hundred years from serfdom; neither they nor their ancestors had ever owned the land they worked on; and they found the present system good.

I learned later that this farm was somewhat above the average in physical equipment. But it was run much like 250,000 other collective farms in the Soviet Union. And I began to realize how the collective farms constituted the very backbone of Russia's tough resistance.

Behind the front in Russia stand the factories and the farms, in a form of total mobilization unknown perhaps anywhere else in the world except in Germany. Behind the factories and the farms stands the machine which keeps this mobilization total.

One of the most interesting and important parts of this machine seemed to me to be the newspapers, like every other part, under government control.

In Moscow, for the first time in my life or in that of Gardner Cowles, Jr., American newspaper publisher, who was with me, we saw men and women standing in queues a block long to buy newspapers. The daily press is published in circulations which run into seven figures but still cannot meet the demand.

In smaller towns throughout Russia, I saw small crowds of people gathered around glass cases set up in the streets. Inside the cases were pinned copies of *Pravda* or *Izvestia,* the country's two leading papers. People wanted to read them enough to stand in the cold and read over other people's shoulders.

When we flew to Tashkent, our airplane made the flight faster than any regular commercial service of the Soviets. As the first Americans who had been seen in that Central Asian city in many years, we were naturally enough objects of considerable curiosity. We were, that is, until it was learned that we had brought more recent copies of the Moscow papers than any Tashkent had seen. At this point, even our official hosts deserted us to read the news.

I was curious about this, and everywhere I went I asked questions about it. The press in Russia, I came to believe, is the strongest single agency in the hands of the government for short-term purposes, just as I believe the schools are their strongest agency over the long pull. The present government of Russia has had both the schools and the press in its control now for twenty-five years, and foreigners who still belittle the strength of this government, in cold, matter-of-fact terms of the support and sacrifices it can demand from the Russian people, are talking through their hats.

One night, in Moscow, I had a chance to check the kind of thinking and emotion that goes into the Soviet press. The American newspapermen in Moscow are as able a group of reporters as I have ever known. Walter Kerr of the *New York Herald Tribune,* Leland Stowe of *The Chicago Daily News,* Maurice Hindus of the *New York Herald Tribune,* Ralph Parker of *The New York Times,* Henry Shapiro of the

United Press, Eddie Gilmore and Henry Cassidy of the Associated Press, Robert Magidoff of the National Broadcasting Company, and Larry Lesueur of the Columbia Broadcasting System, Wally Graebner of *Time* and *Life*—I know no other city in the world, except possibly London, where there is such a company of lively, honest, and hard-working foreign correspondents and newspapermen. Some of them assembled one night a group of Soviet newspapermen, turned us loose in a big room with food and drink and interpreters but no officials, and let me ask the questions I wanted, with no holds barred.

They were an interesting group. There was Ilya Ehrenbourg, Soviet reporter and novelist who has lived most of his life in France and knows western Europe as well, I imagine, as any foreign newspaperman. There was Boris Voitekhov, a young reporter and playwright, who had written the story of the defense of Sevastopol up to the last moment before its fall, when he escaped in a submarine. There was Valentina Genne, a young Soviet newspaperwoman. Simonov was there, a dour-faced young man in Russian *rubashka* and leather boots. He had come to Moscow that day from Stalingrad. He is the author of the play *Russian People,* and perhaps the most popular newspaperman in Russia today. There was General Alexei Ignatiev, a fine figure of a man in his sixties, who served as military attaché abroad before the 1917 Revolution and is now one of the leading commentators of *Red Star,* the daily newspaper of the Red Army.

We ate smoked sturgeon and drank hot tea and talked most of the night. There was two-way traffic in the conversation. They pounded me on the second front in Europe, on what had happened to Rudolph Hess, on the Russian need for more American supplies and equipment. They were well informed, eager, curious, critical but not antagonistic. I was told later that this had been probably the first frank and off-the-record conversation between Soviet newspapermen and a visiting foreigner for a decade.

None of the professional writers present that evening have violated the confidence in which we exchanged opinions. And I shall certainly not do so. But they will not misunderstand, I am certain, if I report for once in my life on some of the things newspapermen told me.

Two things deserve to be reported. The first was what I can only call a quality of intransigence. Those fellows were uncompromising. Train a man from boyhood in a system of absolutism, and he will think in blacks and whites.

For example, I asked Simonov, just returned from Stalingrad, whether or not the German prisoners taken on that front made the same poor and shabby impression I had got from Germans I had interviewed a few days before on the Rzhev front. My question was translated into Russian. But there was no answer. Someone else picked up the ball and carried it.

After living for a few weeks with interpreters, you learn to be surprised at nothing. So I repeated the question. Again, there was no answer. This time I waited until the conversation had come full cycle on itself and reached a pause. I asked the question a third time. General Ignatiev, a courtly and cosmopolitan gentleman and the only Russian

77

present, by the way, who spoke a little English, finally answered me:

"Mr. Willkie, it is only natural that you should not understand. When this war began, we all sought out German prisoners. We cross-examined them. We wanted to find out why they had come to invade our land. We found out many interesting things about the Germans, and about what the Nazis have done to them.

"But now it is different. Since the offensive last winter, when we pushed the Germans back and recaptured many towns and villages they had taken, we feel differently. We have seen with our own eyes what the Germans did to our people and our homes. Today, no decent Soviet newspaperman would talk to a German, even in a prison camp."

Or take another example. I had been suggesting for a few days, as adroitly as I could, that it would be a good move for the Soviets to send Dmitri Shostakovich, their great composer, to the United States on a visit. The night before, I had sat in the packed Tchaikovsky Hall, Moscow's great concert building, and listened to his Seventh Symphony. It is tough music, and much of it is hard for me to like, but its opening movement is one of the most impressive things I have ever heard.

"We have got to understand each other," I said. "We have got to learn to know each other. We are allies in this war, and the American people will not let you down until Hitler has been defeated. But I would like to see us work together in the peace as well as after it. This will require great patience and great tolerance and great understanding on both sides. Why can't Shostakovich be sent to the United States, where he already has a host of admirers and where he could help immeasurably in this job of understanding that we both face?"

It was Simonov who answered me this time.

"Mr. Willkie, understanding works both ways. We have always tried to learn about America. We have borrowed a lot from you, and sent our best men to study in America. We know something about your country, not as much as we would like to but enough to understand why you extend this invitation to Shostakovich.

"You should send some of your good men to study us. Then you would understand why, perhaps, we do not respond warmly to the invitation. You see, we are engaged in a life-and-death struggle. Not only our own lives, but the idea which has shaped our lives for a generation hangs in the balance at Stalingrad tonight. To suggest to us that we should send a musician to the United States, which is also involved in this war and where human lives also hang in the balance, to persuade you with music of something that is as plain as the nose on your face, is in a funny way insulting to us. Please don't misunderstand me."

I don't think I misunderstood him.

The second quality of the evening which deserves reporting was one of calm, quiet, confident pride and patriotism. It is hard for us Americans, who have read more horror stories about Russia than anything else for many years, to realize that a generation is running the Soviet Union today which knows its own strength. I was to be immensely impressed with this later, in central Asia and in Siberia. It is a quality which I have often known in America, especially in the West.

In Moscow I had two long talks with Joseph Stalin. Much of what was said I am not at liberty to report. But about the man himself there is no reason to be cautious. He is one of the significant men of this generation.

At his invitation I called on him one evening at 7:30. He apparently has most of his conferences at night. His office was a fair-sized room about eighteen by thirty-five feet. On its walls hung pictures of Marx and Engels and Lenin, and profiles of Lenin and Stalin together, the same pictures that you see in practically every schoolhouse, public building, factory, hotel, hospital, and home in Russia. Often you find in addition the picture of Molotov. In an anteroom visible from the office was a huge globe some ten feet in diameter.

Stalin and Molotov were standing to welcome me at the far end of a long oak conference table. They greeted me simply and we talked for some three hours—about the war, about what would come after, about Stalingrad and the front, about America's position, the relationship of Great Britain, the United States, and Russia, and about many other important and unimportant subjects.

A few days later I spent some five hours sitting next to Stalin, through the numerous courses of a state dinner which he gave for me; later while we all drank coffee at little tables in another room, and finally through a private showing of a motion picture of the siege and defense of Moscow.

It was at this dinner, incidentally, that we toasted the interpreters. We had toasted our respective countries and leaders; we had toasted the Russian people and the American people and our hopes for future collaboration; we had toasted each other. Finally it occurred to me that the only people really working at that dinner were the interpreters who were kept bobbing up and down to translate. So I proposed a toast to them. Later, I said to Mr. Stalin, "I hope I didn't step out of line in suggesting that we toast the interpreters." And he replied, "Not at all, Mr. Willkie, we are a democratic country."

Stalin, I should judge, is about five feet four or five, and gives the appearance of slight stockiness. I was surprised to find how short he is; but his head, his mustache, and his eyes are big. His face, in repose, is a hard face, and he looked tired in September—not sick, as is so often reported, but desperately tired. He had a right to be. He talks quietly, readily, and at times with a simple, moving eloquence. When he described to me Russia's desperate situation as to fuel, transportation, military equipment, and man power, he was genuinely dramatic.

He has, I would say, a hard, tenacious, driving mind. He asked searching questions, each of them loaded like a revolver, each of them designed to cut through to what he believed to be the heart of the matter that interested him. He pushes aside pleasantries and compliments and is impatient of generalities.

When he asked me about my trips through various factories, he wanted detailed reports, department by department, not general judgments as to their operating methods and efficiency. When I asked him about Stalingrad, he developed for me logically not alone its geographical and military importance, but the moral effect on Russia, Germany, and particularly the Middle East, of the successful or unsuccessful defense. He made no predictions as to Russia's ability to hold it and he was quite definite in his assertion that neither love of homeland nor pure bravery could save it. Battles were won or lost primarily by numbers, skill, and matériel.

He told me again and again that his propaganda was deliberately designed to make his people hate the Nazis, but it was obvious that he himself had a certain bitter admiration for the efficiency by which Hitler had transplanted to Germany as much as ninety-four per cent of the working population from some of the conquered Russian territory, and he respected the completely professional training of the German Army, particularly its officers. He discounted, just as Winston Churchill did to me two years before in England, the notion that Hitler was but a tool in the hands of abler men. He did not think we should count upon an early internal collapse in Germany. He said that the way to defeat Germany was to destroy its army. And he believed that one of the most effective methods of destroying faith in Hitler's invincibility throughout Europe was in continuous air-raid bombings of German cities and of German-held docks and factories in the conquered countries.

When we talked of the causes of the war and the economic and political conditions that would face the world after it was over, his comprehension was broad, his detailed information exact, and the cold reality of his thinking apparent. Stalin is a hard man, perhaps even a cruel man, but a very able one. He has few illusions.

His admiration for the effectiveness of American production methods would more than satisfy the National Association of Manufacturers. But he does not understand the indirections and some of the restraints of the democratic methods of waging war. He wondered, for instance, why the democracies should not insist upon using certain bases for war purposes that would be of great value to them, particularly if the nations that owned them were unco-operative and not able to defend them.

Quite contrary to general report, Stalin has great respect for Winston Churchill; he almost said it to me—the respect of one great realist for another.

On the personal side Stalin is a simple man, with no affectations or poses. He does not seek to impress by any artificial mannerisms. His sense of humor is a robust one, and he laughs readily at unsubtle jokes and repartee. Once I was telling him of the Soviet schools and libraries I had seen—how good they seemed to me. And I added, "But if you continue to educate the Russian people, Mr. Stalin, the first thing you know you'll educate yourself out of a job."

He threw his head back and laughed and laughed. Nothing I said to him, or heard anyone else say to him, through two long evenings, seemed to amuse him as much.

Strange as it may seem, Stalin dresses in light pastel shades. His well-known tunic is of finely woven material and is apt to be a soft green or a delicate pink; his trousers a light-tannish yellow or blue. His boots are black and highly polished. Ordinary social pleasantries bother him a little. As I was leaving him after my first talk, I expressed appreciation of the time he had given me, the honor he conferred in talking so candidly. A little embarrassed, he said:

"Mr. Willkie, you know I grew up a Georgian peasant. I am unschooled in pretty talk. All I can say is I like you very much."

Inevitably, Stalin's simple ways have set a fashion of a kind for other Soviet leaders. Especially in Moscow and in Kuibishev, there is an absence of flamboyance about Russian leaders that is remarkable. They all dress simply. They talk little and listen well. A surprising number of them are young, in their thirties. It would be my guess, which I could not prove or document, that Stalin likes a pretty heavy turnover of young people in his immediate entourage in the Kremlin. It is his way, I think, of keeping his ear to the ground.

Among the other leaders I met and talked to at any great length were Viacheslav Molotov, the Foreign Minister, Andrei Vishinsky and Solomon Lozovsky, his assistants, Marshal Voroshilov, the former Commissar of Defense, Anastasia Mikoyan, Commissar of Supply and head of the Soviet foreign-trade apparatus. Each of these is an educated man, interested in the foreign world, completely unlike in manner, appearance, and speech the uncouth, wild Bolshevik of our cartoons.

84

In Kuibishev, at a dinner given for me by Mr. Vishinsky, who was the chief state prosecutor in all the grim treason trials of four and five years ago, I caught myself studying his white hair, his professor's face, and his quiet, almost studious manner, and wondering if this could possibly be the same man who had purged some of the oldest heroes of the Russian Revolution on charges of murder and betrayal of their country.

Whenever the talk of these men ran to the peace, to what the world must be prepared to do after the war is over, they talked with statesmanship and real understanding.

Since I have returned to the United States, Mr. Stalin has defined the program, as he sees it, of the Anglo-American-Soviet coalition in the European war. These are the goals he calls for:

"Abolition of racial exclusiveness, equality of nations and integrity of their territories, liberation of enslaved nations and restoration of their sovereign rights, the right of every nation to arrange its affairs as it wishes, economic aid to nations that have suffered and assistance to them in attaining their material welfare, restoration of democratic liberties, the destruction of the Hitlerite regime."

We may ask: does Stalin mean what he says? Some will point out that only two years ago Russia was in an alliance of expediency with Germany. I make no defense of expediency, military, political, temporary, or otherwise. For I believe the moral losses of expediency always far outweigh the temporary gains. And I believe that every drop of blood saved through expediency will be paid for by twenty drawn by the sword. But a Russian, feeling that by the German alliance his country was buying time, might well remind the democracies of Munich, and of the seven million tons of the best grade of scrap iron the United States shipped to Japan between 1937 and 1940.

Perhaps we can better measure the good faith of Stalin's statement in the light of the millions of Russians who have already died defending their fatherland and of the sixty million who have become slaves of the Nazis; in those other millions of Russian men and women who are working feverishly sixty-six hours a week in factories and mines to forge and produce instruments of war for the fighters at the front; and in the effort that went into the almost miraculous movement of great factories, hundreds of miles, that they might operate, uninterrupted, beyond Nazi reach. For it is in the attitude of the people that we may find the best interpretation of Stalin's purpose.

Many among the democracies fear and mistrust Soviet Russia. They dread the inroads of an economic order that would be destructive of their own. Such fear is weakness. Russia is neither going to eat us nor seduce us. That is—and this is something for us to think about—that is, unless our democratic institutions and our free economy become so frail through abuse and failure in practice as to make us soft and vulnerable. The best answer to Communism is a living, vibrant, fearless democracy—economic, social, and political. All we need to do is to stand up and perform according to our professed ideals. Then those ideals will be safe.

No, we do not need to fear Russia. We need to learn to work with her against our common enemy, Hitler. We need to learn to work with her in the world after the war. For Russia is a dynamic country, a vital new society, a force that cannot be bypassed in any future world.

5

The Republic of Yakutsk

THE SOVIET UNION covers an enormous territory, bigger than the United States, Canada, and Central America combined. The people are of many different races and nationalities, speaking many languages.

In a Siberian republic called Yakutsk, I found some answers to some of the questions Americans ask about Russia.

Many of the things I saw in Yakutsk would not hold true for all of Russia. Frontier conditions, a cold climate, endless new land free for the asking, and a pioneering spirit among the people are not to be found all over the Soviet Union. But in spite of these differences, Yakutsk—the story of its past and what I saw of its present—taught me new things about the Russian Revolution.

Yakutsk is a big country. It is twice as big as Alaska. It has not many people, only about 400,000 now, but it has resources enough to support a great many more. The Soviets have begun to develop this country, and what I saw of their efforts seemed to me far more important, to the world and to America, than the political debate which has been carried on, both in Moscow and in New York, for so many years.

First, consider the past history of Yakutsk. The Yakuts were Mongol people who spread north as Genghis Khan moved to the west. Their characteristic high cheekbones, slanting eyes, and black hair still persist. Most of them trapped for furs or picked the earth for gold. They lived in huts, low-ceilinged, dirt-floored, smoky from open fires, with cattle and human beings living under the same roof, breeding places for tuberculosis. In winter, they lived on spoiled fish and roots; disease and frequent famines decimated what was once a hardy people. During the time of the tsars, Yakutsk was famous for syphilis, tuberculosis, and furs.

Russians came into this country slowly, and until recently in no great numbers. The government at St. Petersburg (now Leningrad) sent many of its convicts and political prisoners to Yakutsk.

Many writers who had endured its bitter life wrote of it when they were released. And so Yakutsk was known as "the people's prison."

Incidentally, in the waitresses who served us while we were there I found some present-day exiles of the Soviet Union. One Polish woman particularly poured into my ear an account of the Soviet system which hardly accorded with official propaganda.

The first September snow had already coated the airfield when our Liberator bomber landed at Yakutsk, capital city of this republic. We had been flying for hours over the *taiga*, or forestland, which covers the northern part of Siberia as far as the Arctic Circle. The land looks big and cold and empty from the air, with few roads to be seen, and miles upon miles of snow and trees.

A man stepped forward from the small group standing at the edge of the field where our plane stopped.

"My name is Muratov," he said. "I am president of the Council of People's Commissars of the Yakutsk Autonomous Soviet Socialist Republic. I have instructions from Moscow, from Comrade Stalin, to take care of you while you are here, to show you anything you want to see, to answer any questions you may care to ask. Welcome."

It was a short speech, but he gave it everything he had. There were fewer than a dozen men standing on the airfield, but he carried himself with the air of a man flanked by brass bands and guards of honor to welcome a foreign visitor.

I thanked him and explained that we were stopping only briefly as there was still time that day to cover the next thousand-mile lap of our journey.

"You are not going on today, Mr. Willkie," he replied, "nor probably tomorrow. The weather reports are not good and it is part of my instructions to assure your safe arrival at your next stop, or I shall be liquidated."

We drove the five miles or more into the town of Yakutsk in a heavy black Soviet limousine. During the ride Muratov started on the program of selling me his republic, which he never let up on for a moment during the hours I was with him. His enthusiasm knew no subtleties.

"What would you like to see in Yakutsk, Mr. Willkie?" he asked as we neared the town.

"Have you a library?"

"Certainly we have a library."

We went directly to it, and Muratov led us straight to the reading room without stopping for the removal of coats or hats. We were held up at the door, however, by a mild-mannered, slight, studious-looking woman who was completely unabashed by Muratov's obviously official manner. She said politely but firmly, "We are trying to teach the people here not only the habit of reading but the habit of good manners. Please go downstairs and leave your hats and coats in the coatroom." Muratov, a little startled, began to argue, but the best he accomplished was the concession that we might leave our hats and coats in her office. I almost laughed aloud. It was the first and only time in all of Russia that I saw an important Russian official stopped in his stride.

In an old but well-lighted building, clean and well staffed, Yakutsk, a town of 50,000 people, has accumulated 550,000 volumes. The stacks were wooden; the machine for delivering books to the reading room worked like a primitive country well. But the reading room was well occupied. The card catalogues were modern and complete. The records showed that over 100,000 people—many had come from the countryside around—had used books during the past nine months. Special exhibits hung on the walls. Soviet periodicals and reference works were on open shelves. There was an air of great efficiency about the place. This was a library any town of its size might well be proud of.

Our hotel—the only hotel in Yakutsk—was a new building, made of logs, with a Russian stove in every room. It was filled with tough-looking men in leather coats and boots made of reindeer fur. The girls were red-cheeked, with handkerchiefs tied around their heads. They had an amusing way of looking straight at us and laughing their heads off. We were foreigners.

The town itself seemed, in many ways, like a western town in this country a generation ago. In fact, much of this life reminded me of our own early and expanding days—especially the hearty, simple tastes, the not too subtle attitudes of mind, the tremendous vitality. The pavements along the bigger streets were boardwalks, like those I remember in Elwood when I was a boy. The houses had the neat, buttoned-up look of homes in any northern town, with light from the windows and soft smoke coming from the chimneys.

There was plenty to remind us, however, that this was Siberia and not Minnesota or Wisconsin. Most of the houses were built of logs, with felt packed between them, and their façades were covered with the intricate scrollwork of all Siberian houses.

The food was Siberian—a whole roast pig on the table for breakfast, sausages, eggs, cheese, soup, chicken, veal, tomatoes and pickles, wine and a vodka concentrate so strong that even Russians poured water into it. Each meal served to us was as big as the one that preceded it. There was vodka at breakfast, and steaming tea all day long. It is a cold country, and whatever the Yakuts ate outside our hotel, they apparently ate plenty.

I wondered about the amusements of the people.

"Have you a theater?" I asked Muratov.

He had, and we went to it later in the evening. He told me the performance began at nine o'clock. After dinner we drank vodka and talked, and I suddenly realized that it was already after nine.

"What time did you say the show started?" I asked him.

"Mr. Willkie," he answered, "the show starts when I get there."

And so it did. This time nobody stopped him. We walked into our box a half-hour later, sat down, and up went the curtain. We saw a gyspy opera, performed by a Leningrad company on tour. The dancing was excellent, the staging good, the singing fair. The audience liked it noisily, though the theater was not quite filled, this being the ninth consecutive performance of the same opera in that town.

The war was far removed that night from this audience of young people, and so was the ideology of Communism. Love and jealousy and gypsy dances filled the stage, and between the acts the young men with their girls paraded arm in arm around the theater as Russian audiences always do.

But earlier, in the twilight, with the new snow crunching under our feet, we had gone to see the district museum. There we found vivid reminders of the war. The graphs on the walls showing the increase in schools, hospitals, cattle, retail trade, all stopped at June, 1941, as if the country's life had stopped then. And the answer to each of my questions

ended with an explanation of how much more could have
been done had not the Germans put a temporary end to all
normal progress.

Muratov showed me at the museum samples of the real gold
which is now the greatest wealth of Yakutsk, and of the "soft
gold"—or furs—which is its second most valuable product.
Among the sables, foxskins, and bearskins were the soft,
small pelts of Arctic hares and white squirrels. These smaller
animals, he explained, must be shot through the eye if the
skin is not to be spoiled. When I expressed a polite skepticism of the economic possibilities of a profession in which
you must shoot squirrels invariably through the eye, Muratov stood his ground. All Yakutsk hunters, he said, when
they are mobilized into the Red Army, are so good that they
are classified automatically as snipers.

During the day, too, we were aware of the war. Though
Yakutsk is three thousand miles from the front, we found
simple people, most of whom had never seen a German in
their lives or traveled west of the Ural Mountains, talking
earnestly of "the war for the fatherland."

I asked Muratov what he was doing about the education of
the people.

"Mr. Willkie," he said, "the answer is simple. Before 1917,
only two per cent of all the people of Yakutsk were literate;
ninety-eight per cent could not read or write. Now the
figures are exactly reversed.

"Moreover," he went on, smiling cheerfully at me, "I have
now received an order from Moscow to liquidate the two
per cent illiteracy before the end of next year."

94

Once more that term "liquidate." It is constantly used in Russia. It can mean the accomplishment of a set task (the task itself has been liquidated), or it can mean imprisonment, exile, or death for incapacity, failure, or deliberate obstruction. I remembered an item that Joe Barnes had read to me from *Pravda*, about the fate of the manager of a collective farm who had just been sentenced to twenty years' imprisonment because one hundred cows had died on his farm. He had failed to liquidate the causes, so he himself had been liquidated, and the government wanted other farm managers to know.

Muratov showed us with pride Yakutsk's newest motion-picture theater. It was one of the concrete buildings with which he has disproved an old belief that only wooden structures could be built on eternally frozen subsoil.

The most attractive building in town, however, housed the local Communist party headquarters. I had often wondered how in actual practice three million Communist party members—that is all there are in Russia, about one and one-half per cent of the population—could impose their ideas and their control on two hundred million. Here in Yakutsk I began to understand the process.

There was no other organized group in the town; no church, no lodge, no other party. Approximately only 750 people, one and one-half per cent of Yakutsk's 50,000, belong to the Communist party and are members of the town's one club. But these 750 include all the directors of factories, managers of collective farms, the government officials, most of the doctors, superintendents of schools, intellectuals, writers, librarians, and teachers. In other words, in Yakutsk as in most communities in Russia, the best-educated, the most alert, the brightest and ablest men of the community are members of the Communist party. Each of these Communist clubs, all over Russia, is part of a tight-knit national organization, of which Stalin is still Secretary General. One can understand why he still prefers that title to any other which he holds. For this organization keeps the party in power. Its members are the vested-interest group. That is the answer.

Americans would not like that kind of one-party system. But I found in Yakutsk evidence of one of the Soviet Union's greatest achievements and one which the best and most progressive Americans must applaud: its handling of the terrible problem of national and racial minorities.

This town is still largely populated by Yakuts. They made up eighty-two per cent of the population of the republic. As far as I could see, they lived as the Russians lived; they held high office; they wrote their own poetry and had their own theater. Appointive offices filled from Moscow, like Muratov's, were more often held by Russians. Elective offices were usually filled, I was told, by Yakuts. Schools taught both languages. War posters along the streets were captioned in both Russian and Yakut.

How permanent this solution will be it would be hard to predict. Undoubtedly some of its strength lies in the great open spaces of a republic so big that most of it is still unmapped, where more than 100,000 different lakes and streams, Muratov told me, have in the last few years been found and named. I realize that empty space such as we flew over in the republic of Yakutsk for two long days is a great cushion for the conflicts which in Europe have bred prejudice and persecution.

Few things in this Siberian outpost of the Soviet Union interested me more than Muratov himself. If the town of Yakutsk suggested answers to many of my questions, Muratov gave me the key to many others. For he is typical of the new men who are running Russia. And many of his characteristics and much of his career were curiously like those of many Americans I have known.

He is a short, stocky man, with a round, smiling, clean-shaven face. Born in Saratov on the Volga, he was the son of a peasant farmer. Picked from a machine shop in Stalingrad for special schooling because he was bright, he had worked and studied his way through school, through the university, and through the Institute of Red Professors, Moscow's leading graduate school in the social sciences. Two years ago, he had been sent here close to the Arctic Circle to head the Council of People's Commissars of Yakutsk.

Here he was, thirty-seven years old, educated entirely after the 1917 Revolution, running a republic bigger than any other in the U.S.S.R., more than five times as big as France. I saw a good deal of him for a couple of days. He is a man who would do well in America; in his own country he was doing something more than well.

His way of doing things, like the Soviet way all over Siberia, is rough and tough and often cruel and sometimes mistaken. His comment would be: "But it gets results."

97

When I pressed him for details about the economic development of Yakutsk, he talked like a California real-estate salesman. And once more I was reminded of the robust days of great development in this country, at the beginning of the century, when our own leaders were men chiefly interested in getting things done.

"Why, consider, Mr. Willkie. We set up the Yakutsk Autonomous Soviet Socialist Republic in 1922, when the civil wars were finally won. Stalin was Commissar of Minor Nationalities then. Since that time, we've multiplied the budget of this republic eighty times, and everyone who lives here knows it in his heart and in his stomach.

"Why, Yakutsk used to be just a white spot on all the maps. Now, this month, our gold mines won third place in competing against all the nonferrous mining of Russia. They are ahead of plan." And he filled me with figures.

His power plant had just won first place in a competition of all municipal plants in the Soviet Union, and a red flag from the party for cutting production costs to 6.27 kopecks for each kilowatt hour.

"We've invested more than a billion rubles in Yakutsk in twenty years," he said. "We'll cut nearly 4,000,000 cubic meters of wood this year, against 35,000 in 1911. And we've still got a long way to go before we hit the annual growth, which we figure is 88,000,000 cubic meters."

He had obviously been planning in terms of international trade.

"When this war is over, you in America are going to need wood and wood pulp. And we're going to need machines, all kinds of machines. We're not so far away from you, as soon as we get the Arctic sea route open. Come and get it; we'll be glad to swap."

I saw with my own eyes that his tales were not all salesmanship. Yakutsk is about a thousand miles from a railroad. Only this year they are finishing a hard-surfaced, all-weather highway to tie the republic in with the Trans-Siberian Railroad and Moscow. Until now, they have been dependent for communication on airways and on the Lena River. In summer, steamers and barges move goods up the Lena to Yakutsk from Tikhsi Bay, where the Arctic freighters berth. In winter, the river's frozen surface makes the only hard road the republic has ever known.

Gold and furs are precious goods; they have moved without roads since the beginning of history. But Yakutsk has now been found by Soviet research expeditions to have great wealth in other things: silver, nickel, copper, lead. Oil has been found, and although details of the wells are military secrets, Muratov told me they would be producing commercially before the end of 1943. In fish, lumber, and salt, the country has literally untapped resources. And a sizable ivory industry has been built, curiously enough, on the tusks of mammoths, prehistoric animals which once ranged over this area and have been preserved ever since in Arctic cold storage.

Even in agriculture, Yakutsk has possibilities. At the museum, they showed me samples of the crossbred wheat with which the Russians have been pushing northward the limit of their wheat belt. The growing season is short, but the subsoil is full of water and the sun shines all day and almost all night in summer.

Most of the farms—ninety-seven per cent in September—have been collectivized. Reindeer are still the chief motive power of the republic, but there are now some hundreds of tractors, operated from machine tractor stations which lease them to the farms. The republic even has 160 combines—"Think of it, Mr. Willkie, 160 combines at the Arctic Circle!"—and a small but growing army of specialists determined to make the frozen tundra of the north flower and produce crops.

These people have developed an enthusiasm and a self-confidence which reminded me repeatedly of the romance of our own Western development. I came away from Yakutsk with a powerful curiosity to know what it will look like ten years from now.

When I got home, I found a similar curiosity about all Russia in people's minds and an attitude toward Russia made up of admiration and fear.

What is Russia going to do? Is she going to be the new disturber of the peace? Is she going to demand conditions at the end of the war that will make it impossible to re-establish Europe on a decent peaceful road? Is she going to attempt to infiltrate other countries with her economic and social philosophy?

Frankly, I don't think anyone knows the answers to these questions; I doubt if even Mr. Stalin knows all the answers.

Obviously, it would be ridiculous for me to attempt to

say what Russia is going to do. This much, however, I do know to be true: there are 200,000,000 subjects of the U.S.S.R.; they control the largest single land mass in the world under one government; they have almost inexhaustible supplies of timber, iron, coal, oil, which are, practically speaking, unexploited; through elaborate systems of hospitalization and public-health organizations the Russian people are one of the healthiest peoples in the world, living in a vigorous, stimulating climate; in the last twenty-five years, through a widespread, drastic educational system, a large percentage have become literate and tens of thousands technically trained; and from the topmost official to the most insignificant farm or factory worker the Russians are fanatically devoted to Russia and supercharged with the dream of its future development.

I don't know the answers to all the questions about Russia, but there's one other thing I know: that such a force, such a power, such a people cannot be ignored or disposed of with a high hat or a lifting of the skirt. We cannot act as if we were housewives going into an A & P store, picking and choosing among the groceries displayed; taking this, leaving that. The plain fact is: we have no choice in the matter. Russia will be reckoned with. That is the reason why I am constantly telling my fellow Americans: work in ever-closer co-operation with the Russians while we are joined together in the common purpose of defeating a common enemy. Learn all we can about them and let them learn about us.

There's still another thing I know: geographically, from

a trade standpoint, in their similarity of approach to many problems, the Russians and the Americans should get along together. The industrialization of Russia will require a limitless amount of American products, and Russia has unlimited natural resources that we need. The Russians, like us, are a hardy, direct people and have great admiration for everything in America, except the capitalistic system. And, frankly, there are many things in Russia that we can admire —its vigor, its vast dreams, its energy, its tenacity of purpose. No one could be more opposed to the Communist doctrine than I am, for I am completely opposed to any system that leads to absolutism. But I have never understood why it should be assumed that in any possible contact between Communism and democracy, democracy should go down.

So let me say once more: I believe it is possible for Russia and America, perhaps the most powerful countries in the world, to work together for the economic welfare and the peace of the world. At least, knowing that there can be no enduring peace, no economic stability, unless the two work together, there is nothing I ever wanted more to believe. And so deep is my faith in the fundamental rightness of our free economic and political institutions that I am convinced they will survive any such working together.

6

China Has Been Fighting Five Years

IF WE ARE to win a true victory in this world war in which we are now engaged, we must have a clear understanding of the people of the Far East. In our first year of direct fight, ing, most Americans have come to realize that the war in Asia is no sideshow to the war in Europe. But if we hope to prevent war in the future, we must know what are the forces at work in this vast area of the world. We shall need to know those which are friendly to us, and we shall need to be honest enough to back them, no matter what this may mean to many of our conventional prejudices about the world.

It was because I felt deeply our new involvement with the Far East that I made up my mind to go to China. For a few days after the trip was first discussed in Washington, it seemed that transport difficulties, in view of the President's expressed desire that I should not go to India, might make this extremely hard. But these were cleared up before we left New York.

I lunched in Washington with T. V. Soong, China's Foreign Minister, a few days before I left. He spoke to me openly and frankly about his country's difficulties, both financial and military, and his hopes for a real coalition strategy of the United Nations. Only such a strategy, he thought, could help China, and could make the tremendous potential weight of the democracies effective on the same extensive scale as that on which Hitler and General Tojo make their plans.

I agree with him. But neither my trip to China nor the subsequent history of attempts to forge a real coalition strategy bringing China and Russia into full and unequivocal alliance with Great Britain and America has yet given me any substantial reassurance on this score. The tendency of many of our leaders to let the war fall apart into a first-class war and a second-class war still frightens me. Certainly my trip to the Far East left no doubt in my own mind about this. Either we win the war in full partnership with the Chinese in Asia, as with the British and the Russians and the occupied nations in Europe, or we shall not really have won it.

I know there are many who believe that the way to control the future is largely through Anglo-American dominance. They expect an eventual invasion of western Europe by Great Britain and the United States, when Germany becomes sufficiently softened, and an occupation of the Middle East by their combined forces. Thus, they figure, Russia's advances and future dominance will be offset by our occupation of western Europe, with the consequent rallying of the conquered peoples to our standards. They likewise, after Hitler is disposed of, visualize the United States and Great Britain as jointly, with some help from China, destroying Japan. They see after the war a China, treated kindly, intact but weak, and the forces of Asia paternalistically directed for the good of the East by the Western powers, in the ways that seem best for future world peace and security. They think of control of the world's strategic military and trade points as an Anglo-American trusteeship for East and West alike, guaranteed by superior Anglo-American strength. Thus the Western cultural and political values will be preserved, peace restored, economic security provided, and all the world brought to our enlightened standards of democracy and well-being.

It's a persuasive argument. It sounds good—provided you ignore the noble expressions of the Atlantic Charter which President Roosevelt—not Prime Minister Churchill—has specifically extended to the peoples of the Pacific; provided you ignore the preachments of the Four Freedoms with which we have been trying to indoctrinate the world; provided you forget the thinking of about two billion people.

For many years we have lived in ignorance of the true ambitions and capabilities of Japan and its appeal to the growing aspirations of the East for a place in the sun. We have underrated the Japanese, as a result, and disregarded the developing forces in the East. We knew vaguely that the Japanese were trying to build an empire. We are only now beginning to realize how great that empire would be if it were built.

Japan's dreams have at last taken on reality to our eyes, for we have seen the Japanese conquer a great part of the empire they planned. Besides Korea and Manchuria they hold the entire coast of China. They hold most of the Philippines. They have conquered virtually all the East Indies. They have taken half of Burma and cut the Burma Road. They control at least the eastern half of the Indian Ocean and are knocking on the very doors of Calcutta.

They have gone far enough, indeed, for us to grasp a picture of what the world would be like if they should succeed. Suppose, for instance, that India should fall. Suppose that China, cut off from all aid, should be strangled and conquered. I do not believe that these things are going to happen, but to deny them as *possibilities* is simply to repeat the tragic mistakes of the past.

If all this were to come about, we should witness the creation, not merely of a great empire, but of perhaps the biggest empire in history; an empire composed of about a billion people living on approximately fifteen million square miles of land; an empire occupying one third of the earth and including one half of its total population. That is the Japanese dream.

Moreover, this empire would include within itself almost every resource that can be imagined. It would be self-sufficient, whether for peacetime industry or for war. Japan would then have iron from the Philippines, copper from the Philippines and Burma, tin from Malaya, oil from many islands, chrome, manganese, antimony, bauxite for aluminum, and more rubber than she could ever use. Then it would not be the United States that would be known as the bountiful land, but the so-called Greater East Asia Co-Prosperity Sphere.

I have unbounded faith in the courage, the enterprise, and the destiny of the American people. But I believe that if Americans were forced to live hereafter face to face with an empire of such dimensions, our way of life would be little better than an armed camp, and our vaunted freedom would be little more than a fond hope. We should live in continual alarm, in endless war, under crushing armaments which it would be our constant endeavor to increase. Neither peace nor prosperity, neither freedom nor justice, could flourish in such a struggle for existence. And it would not matter in the least how wide or how narrow the Pacific Ocean is.

I believe that we are going to avoid that calamity. I believe we are going to avoid it by striking hard, over and over again, before it is too late. But striking alone will not be enough. We must come to a better understanding of what is happening in the East, of the views of its people, of the changes that have taken place in their ways of thinking, of their loss of faith in Western imperialism, and in the superiority of the white man, and their desires for freedom, according to their standards and ideals. We all say that this is a "war for men's minds," a political war. But too often, as in North Africa and in the East, we perform in terms of old power politics and purely military operations, in terms of expediency and apparent practicalities. We too frequently forget what the war is about and too easily abandon our ideals. We do not keep sufficiently in our active consciousness that it might already be too late to defeat Japan's super-empire either militarily or politically, had it not been for the desperate resistance of the Chinese people through five long, heartbreaking years.

It is not particularly pleasant for Americans to look back across the last five years during which so few realized the importance to our entire civilization of the Chinese resistance. It was not a particularly pleasant thing for me to think about while I was in China, talking to the men who had led and carried out that resistance. While we were absorbed in our bitter quarrels and isolationist delusions, we never took time to understand the heroic role that the Chinese were playing, let alone to send them substantial help. Now we are in a great war to retrieve that error. We must retrieve it.

The Chinese outlook on the future is almost the opposite of that of the Japanese. They do not seek empire. They seek merely to hold and to develop their own vast and lovely homeland. They want to see the new forces that are stirring in the East used for their own freedom and for the freedom of other peoples. Meanwhile the Japanese seek to use the same forces for their imperialistic designs.

China is much larger than the United States, both in area and in population. It contains within its boundaries many rich resources. On the other hand, it is not self-sufficient—and neither are we. This fact does not disturb the Chinese or make them want to conquer the world, any more than it does us. Self-sufficiency is a delusion of the totalitarians. In a truly democratic world, a nation would have no more need of self-sufficiency than the state of New York has of making itself independent of the state of Pennsylvania.

We must not expect Chinese ideas of personal liberty and democratic government to be exactly the same as ours. Some of their ideas may seem to us too radical, others may seem ridiculously archaic. We should remember that in their eyes some of *our* customs appear ridiculous and even distasteful. We must keep our minds fixed upon the essential fact that the Chinese want to be free—free in their own way to govern their lives for the benefit and happiness of their own people. They want a free Asia.

The recent treaties between the United States and China and between Great Britain and China, in which extra-territoriality has been given up by us, are a step toward recognition of China's determination to be free. No longer will Americans and Englishmen in China be exempt from Chinese laws and Chinese courts, any more than Chinese in the United States are exempt from American legal processes. But it must not be assumed that these treaties solve the problem. The British, for example, still claim Hong Kong, one of the great ports through which the people of China must trade with the world. And Hong Kong, like the claims of Americans and other nationals in the International Settlement at Shanghai, is only a symbol to the Chinese of the foreign rights and privileges which still bar their way to real freedom.

It is unfortunate that so many Americans still think of China in terms of great inert masses and not in terms of people, still think of the death of five million Chinese as something different from and less costly than the death of five million Westerners. Perhaps the most significant fact in the world today is the awakening that is going on in the East. Even if we win this war militarily, this awakening will still have to be reckoned with. If we are wise, we can direct forces which are in being throughout the East toward world co-operative effort for peace and economic security. These same forces, however, if they are flouted or ignored, will continue to disturb the world.

7

The Opening Up of China's West

I SHALL ALWAYS be glad that I entered China, on my first visit to that country, not through what used to be called a "treaty port," but through the back door, the vast hinterland of China's northwest. The "treaty ports" on the Pacific —all of which are now held by the Japanese—are symbols to the modern Chinese mind of the generations in which China was regarded by Western nations as a large but primitive country to be converted, exploited, or laughed at. Shanghai, Hong Kong, and Canton may be beautiful cities; but to the Chinese even their names are reminders of the days when, as Sun Yat-sen, founder of the Chinese Republic, put it, "the rest of mankind is the carving knife and the serving dish, while we are the fish and the meat."

Instead, my first stop in China was at Tihwa, called by the Russians Urumchi, capital city of the province of Sinkiang, or Chinese Eastern Turkistan. Our Liberator had flown from Tashkent in Siberia in a single day. Most of the flight had been down the Ili River valley which cuts between some of the highest mountain ranges in the world—the Tien Shan and the Altai Mountains. For hours we flew over empty desert, as strangely beautiful as any landscape I have ever seen, before we came down on the fertile land of grapes and melons which is called by the Chinese Sinkiang, or "New Dominion."

Sinkiang is twice as big as France. It has something less than 5,000,000 inhabitants. It is the largest province of China and may conceivably be the richest. It is not only close to the geographical center of Asia, but also close to its political center, for it is here that Russia and China meet. Over the long pull, what happens in this strange territory, about which many Americans have never heard, may have decisive influence on our history.

Very few foreigners have been there in the last generation. When I was in Tihwa, my Chinese hosts estimated that only a few dozen American or English travelers had flown through Sinkiang on the Chinese-Russian commercial airline which operated between China and Moscow until a year ago. Even these few saw more of Hami, a smaller town with a better airport, than they did of the capital, Tihwa.

The town itself has little to boast of. It is small, sleepy-looking, and incredibly muddy. The street signs are in Russian, the government is Chinese, the people are Turkis, part of the 20,000,000 Moslems who live inside the frontiers of China. It boasts the finest melons in Asia and some small, seedless grapes as good as any I have ever eaten. The mountains around the town are filled with metals. Irrigation gives the province its food; its only export of importance at present is wool, which now goes in substantial quantities to help clothe the Red Army.

Sinkiang is one of the areas in the world where politics and geography combine to make a kind of explosive amalgam full of meaning to those who are curious about what is going to happen to the world. Geography leans Sinkiang toward Russia. The Soviet Turk-Sib Railroad runs a few miles from its frontier. All the consumers' goods we saw in Tihwa came from Russia; the cars we rode in were Russian; the army we saw drove Russian tanks. But politics leans the province back toward China. Chinese have ruled Sinkiang since the Han dynasty. The present governor is Chinese. And now the desperate, hopeful drive in China to open up its own hinterland has blown like a fresh wind through the province. Soviet-Chinese relations will be important to the whole world after this war, and they may be determined in this area.

The Soviet government has always recognized Chinese sovereignty over Sinkiang. There has never been anything like a border clash between the two nations. But the pressure of railroads, markets, commercial credits, Communist ideology, has swung the province steadily into a Soviet orbit during the last ten years, and if the Chinese set up a countervailing pressure by industrializing and developing their northwest provinces, including Sinkiang, it will mean a real test of the strength of two powerful peoples.

I heard tales, both in Moscow and in Chungking, of political difficulties in Sinkiang which bordered on straight fiction. One of the chief actors in the plot, Ma Chung-ying, a Chinese Moslem leader who invaded Sinkiang from the neighboring province of Kansu in 1932, with a Robin Hood reputation and a great way with his fellow Moslems, walked across the frontier in 1934 and is rumored to be in Moscow today, waiting his time to go back. Another chief leader is Sheng Shih-tsai, now Governor of Sinkiang, a Chinese. Since he is a native of China's northeastern provinces of Manchuria, occupied by the Japanese since 1931, he is bitterly anti-Japanese. His brother was found killed in his bed in the Governor's palace last June, and the legends which pass as news in Asia have it that Russians were accused of complicity in his murder.

I could not learn what truth there was in the stories. Probably there was none. I dined with Governor Sheng in Tihwa, and the Soviet Consul General dined with us. We toasted each other and the three countries from which we came in Russian vodka and in Chinese rice wine, and there was no hint of anything but cordial friendship between Russia and China. But the next morning I had a private breakfast, at his suggestion, with the Chinese Governor, who once was sympathetic with the Communists and of late has shifted his allegiance to the Generalissimo. The stories he told me of murder, intrigue, espionage, and counterespionage sounded like a dime thriller and would have been incredible to an American were it not for the evidence all about of suspicion and mystery. Obviously, one of our problems, when the war is over, will be to help China and Russia work out in co-operation the common problems they face in Turkistan, near the roof of the world in Asia.

And that is another reason why I urge and urge again the necessity of bringing China and Russia, the United States and Great Britain, in common conference today to learn to work with each other while they fight. For if they do not there is enough explosive powder in Central Asia to blow the lid off the world again when the present fighting is over.

Governor Sheng's dinner was not only the first of a long series of Chinese banquets given for me by what must certainly be the most hospitable people in the world. It was also one of the most interesting. We sat in a long, vaulted room with men facing each other across narrow tables running down both sides of the hall. The walls were covered with inscriptions of welcome to an American, of challenge to our common enemies, of faith in our victory, written in the seventeen languages which pass currency in that crossroads of Asia where one of the oldest caravan routes in the world still links Europe and Asia.

The Governor is a tall man with handsome, black mustaches. He is a Manchurian, Chinese in origin, and has studied in Japan. He has been Governor of Sinkiang for more than ten years and knows the country well, with its intrigue and conflicting forces. I had talked with him in his office in the afternoon, and he had told me of the problems of running a province which is forty-six days' travel from his nation's capital.

In Tihwa, as in every other Chinese city I was to visit, I was given really moving evidence of the good will with which Americans are regarded all over the world. Nothing could have been farther from that banquet hall on that September night than the United States. Even our fellow diners, officials and army officers for the most part, looked at me with curiosity which suggested that many of them were seeing an American for the first time in their lives. Yet there was a warmth and a friendliness in their reception of me which spoke eloquently of their unspoken hope that the United States will continue to be China's friend in the years to come.

Everything about Tihwa reminded us, more vividly than Tashkent or Teheran or Bagdad, of the real vitality and strength of Asia. The next day, the Governor staged a military review for his American visitors. On a big parade ground, we watched the Sinkiang army, or what must have been a very large part of it, file past in dress parade.

It was a fascinating show. The soldiers looked neat, well trained, and healthy. Their equipment was limited in amount, but most of it seemed to be Russian and good. They had mobile artillery, machine guns mounted on motorcycles, scout cars with armor, a few light but fast tanks. There were several contingents of truck-borne infantry. The Russian origin of the equipment became only too clear when one artillery regiment galloped by us with *kachankas,* the Ukrainian farm wagons with machine guns mounted on them which were first developed by guerrillas in the Soviet civil wars and which have now played an important part in holding the Nazis in the Ukraine a second time.

But the climax of the show was strictly local. Several dozen cavalrymen, lithe, wiry Mongols and Kazaks who sat their saddles as if they were part of the horses, charged in turn through a series of assignments, perhaps fifteen, any one of which was enough to take your breath away. With two-edged sabers they cut through saplings, sliced off a dummy head, picked objects off the ground—all at a dead gallop. It was not hard to understand, after watching them, the terror Genghis Khan inspired in his enemies.

Generalissimo Chiang Kai-shek had sent a formal welcome to me at Tihwa, brought by two of his closest personal friends and aides, who accompanied me all the rest of the time I was in China. They were Dr. Hollington K. Tong, Vice-Minister of Information, and General Chu Shao-liang, commander in chief of the northwest war zone. Before I left China, I had a deep affection for both of them.

"Holly" Tong had been described to me on my way to China by a foreigner whose knowledge of that country and love for it seemed to me as great as any man's, as "one of the Generalissimo's keenest instruments, as faithful as a dog and as clean as a dog's tooth." He is a graduate of Park College, in Missouri, and of the Columbia School of Journalism in New York. After a distinguished career as a Chinese newspaper publisher, he became one of the Generalissimo's closest advisers, helping to run an important ministry and at the same time serving as translator, secretary, and counselor to his chief. He seemed to me, and I came to know him well, the kind of aide any great leader would like to have.

General Chu, unlike "Holly" Tong, whose English is

amazingly fluent and idiomatic, spoke not one word that I could understand. He made up for it by one of the most endearing personalities I have ever known. I never sat down to a banquet in China, or finished a speech, or walked out of a conference without seeing him smile at me in the friendliest possible way. He talked little, and held himself with the dignity expected of a distinguished soldier who had fought with the Generalissimo through his hardest and earliest campaigns in unifying China, but he did as much as any man could to make me feel that China was not an alien country, full of strange customs, but a warm-hearted, hospitable land filled with friends of America.

Another Chinese whose warm friendliness is hard to forget had traveled with us all the way from Moscow. He was Major Hsu Huan-sheng, an assistant military attaché in the Chinese Embassy at Kuibishev. On some of the flights we made inside China, he piloted the plane. In 1938, three years before the United States went to war, this young fellow, who still looks like a boy of seventeen, had made himself famous by piloting the first Chinese raid over Japan, dropping pamphlets. I was glad that his trip with us gave him a chance to see his wife and children, on our way to the front near Sian, and I was sorry when he left us in Siberia on our way home, to go back to his job.

These men were in our plane when we left the next morning, September 29, to fly to Lanchow, capital of Kansu province. This five-hour flight was from one point of view the most remarkable lap of our flight around the world. While you are flying through a world at war, trying after each stop to prepare yourself to understand the next one, or to steal a little sleep, scenery inevitably plays a secondary role. But the landscape between Tihwa and Lanchow was one of the most amazing sights of my life, and with utter fascination we watched it unfold beneath us.

For straight beauty, it would be hard to beat. Part of the way was over desert, and part over green, cultivated fields. It was all mountainous, but once we had left the snow-covered Tien Shan range behind us, the mountains were lower and surprisingly fertile. In places, the Chinese have terraced the hills right to the top, and the ground below looked like a gigantic billiard table which had been dented into an irregular, infinitely varied, rolling carpet of green.

As we neared Lanchow, we hit the red loam hills from which the wind and the rivers have carried over centuries the soil which now covers most of northern China. These red hills are unbelievably lovely to look at from the air, but I could not see them without thinking what wealth they represented to a nation determined to open up its west. Irrigation projects, power plants, fertile fields and pastures, whole cities could be built in this region, and all the country lacked to build them, it seemed to me, was people.

I don't know how often I thought of this flight during the weeks I was in China. In the first place, the emptiness of this northwestern region makes a striking contrast with the crowded, teeming lands of southern China. In the second place, every Chinese leader I talked to spoke of the northwest and the present struggle to open its riches with transport, co-operatives, and modern science, as China's most fundamental hope in the war against Japan and in the great task of building a strong, modern nation which will follow the peace.

Finally, and most important, I felt in Tihwa and in Lanchow and in the country between those cities a curious resemblance to our own American West in the days when it was being opened up. The people seemed tall and resourceful, a more rugged type than many we saw in the crowded streets of Chengtu or of Chungking. With the Japanese holding all of the coastal half of China, all the great industrial cities and ports, and much of the rich and fertile agricultural land, the Chinese have no alternative now but to open up their own west. But I was glad to find no attitude of sour grapes in the Chinese who are now pioneering in these areas. Instead, they talk big and a little boastfully and very much like the men of my father's generation in the United States.

In Lanchow I visited some of China's industrial co-operatives. I met there the quiet, sincere New Zealander, Rewi Alley, who has made Indusco an international word and a symbol of what can be done by a people determined to lift itself by its own bootstraps. Alley was having difficulties when I saw him; it is my guess that he will continue to have them. But I have no doubt that he and the Chinese Industrial Co-operative movement I saw in China's northwestern provinces are accomplishing an enormous change in the world's economic geography by opening up the heart of Asia.

This economic struggle in which China is now engaged

has been less written about in America than China's military struggle against the Japanese invaders. But everything I saw made me believe that it has been no less heroic. If we Americans were blasted from our seacoasts by a hostile force, we could retire into our great interior and find there the machines and the skilled labor to fight on. But in the vast interior of China there were no such facilities. The Chinese had to carry their factories inland with them; not on freight cars, not on trucks, not even in carts, but on human backs, piece by heavy piece. They carried them up the great river valleys and across the mountain ranges.

They set them down and put them together in the remote highlands, where the whir of machinery had never been heard. From the relatively few factories that could thus be transported, there have now blossomed more than a thousand industrial establishments—small for the most part, and limited in the scope of their manufactures, but each contributing its bit to the foundation of the new China.

Surely we Americans can read the handwriting on the wall. The opening up of this new China compares only, in modern history, with the opening up of our own West. We know the struggle of those people. We know the hope. And in some significant measure we know what the fulfillment can be. The economic aim of the leaders of modern China is to develop their country much as we developed ours. They want to create an industrial foundation with which to raise the standard of living of their people. Many experts believe that the industrialization of China, once started, will proceed even faster than ours did. The new China starts with advanced technologies. Where we had to await the slow development of the locomotive, they can begin with the three-hundred-mile-an-hour airplane.

So far, they have neither airplanes nor locomotives. In Lanchow I saw the terminal of the Russian highway, the one land route into modern China. I wish every American could see it who has wondered whether there was too much salesmanship in the few stories which have been brought back from China of the heroism and the fortitude with which the Chinese people are still fighting back after more than five years of war against the Japanese.

We had flown over stretches of this highway ever since we crossed the Soviet border, east of Alma-Ata. Alma-Ata is a big city, linked by rail and by airlines to the industries and the raw materials of Siberia, of Soviet Central Asia, and of Russia itself. From Alma-Ata, heavy trucks pound eastward along a hard-surfaced road through Tihwa and Hami and up to the western frontier of Kansu province. We flew over these trucks and convinced ourselves that they were as real as they were incongruous on this ancient silk road, perhaps the oldest caravan route in history, along which Marco Polo traveled on his way to ancient Cathay.

The Chinese end of the road, where there is neither road-bed nor gasoline nor trucks, fits much more appropriately the historical traditions of the highway. Instead of trucks, the Chinese use carts, camels, and coolies. Soviet freight, which takes four days from the frontier to the Kansu border, takes seventy more days to reach Lanchow. And still it has not reached a railhead, but must travel days and days farther by the most primitive transport imaginable before it debouches into the heavily populated parts of China where it is so desperately needed.

Outside Lanchow, between the airport and the city, we saw a Chinese caravan being formed for the long haul back toward Russia. It was made up of small, two-wheeled mule carts, rubber-tired—strangely, to my rubber-conscious eyes— and piled high with wool and salt and tea. The mules were standing patiently in a row which must have been some miles long, the coolies next to them, waiting for the order to start. They would be plodding westward for more than two months, I was told, before they could exchange their cargo for the gasoline, airplane parts, engines, and ammunition which the Soviet Union is still shipping to China, largely on credits which have now reached a staggering total.

The road is a shoestring being used to support an enormous weight. If the shoestring breaks, we shall all be the losers. I could get no official figures on the amount of traffic which now travels over the road. But Americans in Lanchow estimated that not more than 2000 tons of freight reach China every month along the 1800-mile highway. This is far below the capacity of the Burma Road, which has been cut by the Japanese. But except for the American airplanes which fly in from India over the Himalayas, and the smuggling which seeps through the entire front against Japan, it is China's only link with the world outside.

Lanchow is on the Yellow River, much nearer its source than Tungkuan, where we were to look across it a week or two later into Japanese encampments. It is a city of roughly half a million people, without a railroad, with no important factory more than six years old, but with a great future. Kansu province, of which it is the capital, is rich land, with enormous possibilities.

It was in Lanchow that General Chu took me to his home to meet his wife. We climbed out of the city up a hill which looks down on the town and the river beyond it. Near the top of the hill is a Chinese temple which serves as headquarters for the military command of the five northwestern provinces of China—Shensi, Kansu, Ninghsia, Chinghai, and Sinkiang. Here we sat and drank tea and ate an enormous cake with the general and Mrs. Chu. From a balcony outside the general's workroom, the view fell over the tiled roofs of the temple buildings, across the town itself, to the river with its irrigation works which have been functioning for two thousands years to make the land of Kansu fertile.

That night we had another banquet, given by Governor Ku Cheng-lun of Kansu, in the Officers' Moral Endeavor Association hostel, where we were put up for the night. There were other dignitaries present besides my host: General Yu Fei-peng, Minister of Transport and Supply, and Admiral Shen Hung-lieh, Minister of Agriculture. They talked about the province's forestry, agriculture, and water-conservancy problems, and its fledgling industries, some of which, including a blanket factory, I saw the next morning. I was still some days away from Chungking, China's wartime capital, but I already began to feel the strength from which this amazing nation has drawn its capacity to fight back against the Japanese.

8

What Free China Fights With

ROM LANCHOW we flew south to Chengtu, then up into
the mountains to the capital, Chungking. On the way
home from China, we flew north to Sian, then back again
to Chengtu to take off on the long flight across north China
and the Gobi to Siberia. With shorter flights to visit American headquarters or army camps in Szechwan or Yünnan,
we covered a substantial portion of the provinces left in
free China still untouched by the Japanese except for bombing raids.

There are ten of these provinces, five in the northwest
and five in the southwest. In the northwest, we had seen the
future of China. In the southwest, especially in Szechwan
province—Chengtu and Chungking—we saw its present at
its best.

Here it was not the land but the people that made the
strongest impression. It is difficult for anyone to understand
fully the inexhaustible human resources of that country.

People who know China but have not been there since 1937, when Japan began its present attempt to conquer China, tell me the vitality, the resourcefulness, the courage and devotion to their cause of freedom which distinguish the Chinese people are a constant marvel to them.

After visiting China's cotton mills, its munitions factories, its pottery works and cement plants, after talking with their managers and with hundreds of their workers for many hours, I began really to appreciate the ingenuity and adaptability of Chinese skill in modern industrial methods. And what is generally spoken of as the awakening of China came to mean something actual to me when I had discussed with college professors and grade-school teachers alike the irresistible urge to shake off the past which has caused modern China in a relatively few years to change literacy from the privilege of the few to the right of the masses. Almost 100,000,000 Chinese are now literate. At the universities learning is no longer measured in terms of pure erudition. Chinese scholars of today apply China's rich lore to the problems of modern life. No longer do they seek only the cloisters; they now compete hotly for better ways to serve society and the state in which they live.

At Chengtu I met and plied with questions the presidents of the eight universities there. The faculties of six had escaped from Japanese-occupied areas and were now using the facilities of the two resident universities in shifts which kept the buildings and the libraries and the laboratories occupied almost twenty-four hours a day.

I shall never forget the impressive scene as I spoke at an

early morning hour to the ten thousand students of those universities and heard their full-throated cheers at every reference to freedom. All over China I talked with men who were responsible for the little schoolhouses where the children of Chinese peasants and coolies for the first time in history have an opportunity to learn.

Where ten years ago there were a hundred newspapers in what is now free China, today there are a thousand. In almost every sizable town there are one or more, and the editorials which were translated for me are pungent and forceful. The Chinese Central News Service in its professional methods of gathering and distributing the news compares well with our own press services and with British Reuter's.

I arrived in Chungking late in the afternoon, at an airport some miles from the city. Long before our automobiles had reached the city, the road on either side was lined with people. Before we reached the middle of the city, the crowds stood packed from curb to store front. Men, women, young boys and girls, bearded old gentlemen, Chinese with fedora hats, others with skullcaps, coolies, porters, students, mothers nursing their children, well dressed and poorly dressed— they packed eleven miles of road over which our cars slowly moved on our way to the guesthouse in which we were to stay. On the other side of the Yangtze River, they stood and waited. On all the hills of Chungking, which must be the world's hilliest city, they stood and smiled and cheered and waved little paper American and Chinese flags.

Any man who has run for President of the United States is used to crowds. But not to this one. I could discount it in my mind as much as I wished, but to no avail. The paper flags waved by the people were all of the same size, suggesting that the hospitable and imaginative Mayor of Chungking, Dr. K. C. Wu, had had a hand in planning this demonstration. It was perfectly clear that not all these people, many of whom were barefoot or dressed in rags, had any clear idea of who I was or why I was there. The firecrackers which were exploding on every street corner, I told myself, are an old Chinese passion, anyway.

But in spite of all my efforts to discount it, this scene moved me profoundly. There was nothing synthetic or fake about the faces I looked at. They were seeing, in me, a representative of America and a tangible hope of friendship and help that might be forthcoming. It was a mass demonstration of good will. And it was an impressive show of the simple strength, in people and in emotions, which is China's greatest national resource.

I had seen a crowd like this one, but a little smaller, on my arrival in Lanchow, far into the northwest. I was later to see another, as impressive as any, which waited for hours in the rain on the streets of Sian, capital of Shensi province, because our plane was late. They never failed to move me deeply. It is impossible in a short trip through a country as big as China to make as many close and personal friendships as one would like, those relationships through which one generally comes to know the spirit and the ideas of a foreign people. But these crowds of Chinese people gave me a sure and lasting feeling that my surface impressions of China were backed by something no one could misread in those thousands of faces.

The Chinese I came to know well were, inevitably, leaders in one field or another. Some of them I will describe later in this account, and in high terms. But I know no praise high enough for the anonymous people of China.

One of them, whom I never met, wrote me a letter while I was in China. He is a student, and he pasted his picture at the end of his letter. His English was the kind that only a student can use who has enormous confidence in himself and in his dictionary.

"Dear Mr. Wendell Willkie," he wrote, "let me assure you that China, one of the bravest and most faithful among the allied countries, has never been daunted or changed her mind while confronting all sorts of hardships; for we perfectly understand that we are fighting for the holy cause of liberty and righteousness, and we firmly believe that a bright future is waiting us ahead, and that God will give us the victory that we ache to get at."

He enclosed a draft plan for the establishment of peace after the war, and it was an interesting plan. But it was the spirit of it which impressed me, like that of the crowds of Chinese I saw everywhere I went. He proposed setting up monuments to make people hate war instead of praising it, and he proposed that the last day of this war should be made a day for public sacrifices all over the world, and be named "Peace, Free, Pleasure Day."

One of the propositions of his plan is called "To increase

the affection among human beings." And he suggested that each nation should raise peace funds with which to endow scientific scholarships. Only science, he wrote me, "can solve the pain of human beings, make up the defects of nature, raise the standard of living of human beings, and make the whole human being struggle with nature but not with mankind."

Possibly no other country on our side in this war is so dominated by the personality of one man as China. His name is Chiang Kai-shek, although he is universally referred to in China as "The Generalissimo," sometimes affectionately shortened to "Gissimo."

I had a number of long talks with the Generalissimo, as well as family breakfasts and other meals alone with him and Mme Chiang.

One late afternoon we drove to the Chiangs' country place, high on the steep bank of the Yangtze River. "Holly" Tong was with us. Across the front of the simple frame house was a large porch where we sat looking out to the hills of Chungking. In the river below, a number of small boats moved in the swift current, carrying the Chinese farmer and his produce downstream to market. It had been a hot day in Chungking but here a pleasant breeze was blowing, and as Mme Chiang served us tea, the Generalissimo and I began to talk, Mme Chiang and "Holly" serving alternately as interpreters.

We discussed the past and his administration's aim to change China from an almost exclusively agricultural society into a modern industrial one. He hoped in the change to retain the best of the old traditions and to avoid the social dislocations of large-scale Western industrial development by the establishment of a great number of widely distributed small plants. He was sure that in the teachings of Dr. Sun, the father of the republic, concerning a combined agricultural and industrial society he would find the way. But he was eager to discuss the question with someone from the West and he asked me many questions. I explained to him that the social problems created by mass production in America and the large industrial combinations which he wanted to avoid had not arisen, as he seemed to think, solely because of desire for power and the building of individual fortunes, though these elements undoubtedly contributed. In part, at least, they arose because of economic requirements: mass production greatly lowers costs.

I gave him the illustration of the automobile, which he hoped to see manufactured at low cost in China to fill Chinese roads. I pointed out to him that an automobile manufactured in a small plant would cost five times as much as an automobile manufactured on an assembly line under scientific management in a large plant. That it is impossible to have some of the products that make for a high standard of living at prices within the reach of the great masses of the people, if they must be produced exclusively in small plants. That every thoughtful American knew that in many instances we have created large industrial combinations unnecessarily. That for our social and economic good we should give the utmost encouragement and preference to the small industries. But that in certain industries, in order to maintain our standard of living, it was necessary to have large-scale production. I told him that we recognized the social, economic, and almost non-democratic maladjustments created by the collection of thousands of workers under single factory roofs, with the consequent possibility of unemployment of whole communities at one time. That we regretted the stratification of large groups of our population into a permanent employee class which this system produced, and the reduction of the opportunity for individual men to become owners of their own businesses. I also told the Generalissimo that we had not as yet found all the answers. But we did know that the solution did not consist in breaking up necessary large units into inefficient small ones.

I reminded him that there was an experiment going on much closer to him than any in the Western world, the Communist one in Russia, and that part of its success was due to the mass-production technique of using large groups for the accomplishment of a particular purpose.

He suggested that perhaps he could find the solution in having necessary large units partly owned by government and partly by private capital.

The discussion went on for hours. Then Mme Chiang, who had been acting as interpreter for us, with pleasant but firm feminine authority, said: "It's ten o'clock and you men haven't had anything to eat. Come on now; we must drive into town and get at least a bite. You can finish this some other time."

At other times we did talk more of this, and of many other things. We talked of India, of the whole East, of its aspirations, of its purposes, of how it should fit into a world-wide order, of military strategy, of Japan and its resources, of Pearl Harbor and the fall of Singapore and their profound psychological effect on the attitude of the East toward the West. We talked of the growing spirit of intense, almost fanatical nationalism which I had found developing in the countries of the Middle East, in Russia and now in China, of how such a spirit might upset the possibility of world co-operation. We talked of Russia and of Chiang's relationship to the Communists within China, of Great Britain and her policy in the East, of Franklin Roosevelt and Winston Churchill and Joseph Stalin.

In fact, the six days I was with the Generalissimo were filled with talk.

I can write no account of China without setting down my own conclusion that the Generalissimo, both as a man and as a leader, is bigger even than his legendary reputation. He is a strangely quiet, soft-spoken man. When he is not in military uniform, he wears Chinese dress, and this accentuates the impression he makes of a scholar—almost a clerical scholar—rather than a political leader. He is obviously a trained listener, used to the task of picking other men's brains. He nods his head when he agrees with you, with continuous soft little ya-ya's; it is a subtle form of compliment, and one that disarms the man he is talking to, and wins him in some degree to Chiang's side.

The Generalissimo is reported to spend a part of every day in praying and Bible reading. He has acquired from this, or from some childhood influence, a reflective manner, a quiet poise, and an occasional appearance of thinking out loud. He is undoubtedly sincere and his dignity and personal imperturbability have something almost severe in quality.

The Generalissimo came to power the hard way, a fact of which he is proud. He has known for more than twenty years the toughest problems of the birth of a nation. His loyalty, perhaps as a result of this, both to the extraordinary family into which he married and to the associates of his early years of struggle, is unbreakable and, I should guess, sometimes unreasonable. I could not document this, but no one can stay in Chungking even for a short time without realizing that the young republic, despite its youth, has already developed a sort of "old-school tie" of its own which automatically keeps some men in high position. The chief wearers of this "old-school tie" are the comrades-in-arms of the Generalissimo during the years when he was fighting warlords, and it is China's gain that none of these is yet an old man.

I would not like to suggest that the leaders I met in Chungking were not men of considerable caliber. They were. But they are not all representative men, in the Western sense. Just as the Chinese concept of democracy differs from ours in certain respects, so does the pattern which life imposes on its leaders. The Kuomintang, the party which rules China, includes in its plan for the growth of self-government in China a tutelary stage during which the people are being educated into new habits of living and thinking designed to make them good citizens of a complete democracy, with electoral rights, at a later time.

During this tutelary stage, it is inevitable that China's leaders should be men with considerable training, either in foreign universities or in war and politics, rather than men chosen by the people primarily to represent them. And so it is. I came to believe in China that this was one factor, and an important one, in the feeling of impatience, which can be found especially in foreign circles not unsympathetic with China, at the centralized control of Chinese life which is exercised in Chungking.

China delegated some of its best men to answer my questions and show me its war effort. It would be impossible to list all of those who made a strong impression on me.

General Ho Ying-chin, Minister of War, gave me a luncheon in his house on the top of a hill in Chungking looking down over the river. I talked then to him, to Lieutenant General Joseph W. Stilwell, to Admiral Chen Shao-kwan, and to other officers of the Chinese Army. Later I had a long discussion with General Pai Chung-hsi, of the Kiangsi triumvirate.

President Lin Sen entertained me formally at his official residence. Dr. H. H. Kung, Vice-President of the Executive Yuan, gave a buffet dinner on the lawn of his home, the finest in Chungking. Dr. Chen Li-fu, Minister of Education, Dr. Wong Wen-hao, Minister of Economics, and Dr. Wang Shih-chieh, at that time Minister of Information, all gave me liberally their time and their services in explaining to me how China was meeting its crisis.

The Generalissimo himself presided at a dinner at the National Military Council, a great hall in the middle of Chungking which had been bombed the year before but was already rebuilt. This was the most appealing public dinner I attended around the world. For it was conducted with the simplicity which one likes to believe exists in high places in these years of necessary sacrifice. The entertainment provided was by musicians playing on instruments of ancient China, many of them one-stringed, and all crude in appearance and construction. But the songs were old Chinese folk songs and the melodies soft.

An episode occurred at this dinner which our party has since remembered with delight. Mike Cowles had been ill the day before, after eating as an experiment some creamed shark's lip. So he was particularly pleased when the dessert at the banquet was good old-fashioned vanilla ice cream. He expressed his pleasure to the Mayor of Chungking, who explained: In April the medical authorities had feared that China would be swept by a cholera epidemic. Since they had no anticholera serum, and since cholera was being spread by milk, they passed a municipal ordinance making it a criminal offense to serve ice cream.

"But," he added, "yesterday I decided that ice cream is such a delicacy and we are so pleased that Mr. Willkie came to Chungking, I just repealed the ordinance for one day so we could serve you ice cream tonight."

For the next few days we waited anxiously to see if our anticholera inoculations were really any good.

There were a great many other Chinese whom I saw in the intervals of time left over by my hospitable hosts, ostensibly for rest. Dr. Soong's home was a convenient meeting place. My curiosity was enormous. The willingness of Chinese to come and be interviewed was without limit.

For instance, it was there that I talked, at leisure, alone and uninterrupted, with Chou En-lai, one of the leaders of the Chinese Communist party. This excellent, sober, and sincere man won my respect as a man of obvious ability. He lives in Chungking, where he helps to edit a Communist newspaper, the *Hsin Hua Jih Pao,* and takes his full part in the meetings of the People's Political Council, China's closest approximation at present to a representative legislative body, of which both he and his wife are members.

I saw General Chou again—he won the rank of general in the civil wars fighting against the Generalissimo on the side of the Communists—at Dr. Kung's dinner party, to which he was invited with his wife, at my suggestion. I was later told that it was the first time he had been entertained by the official family of China. It was interesting to see him greeted in a pleasant but somewhat cautious manner by men he had fought against, and with obvious respect by General Stilwell, who had known him in Hankow ten years ago.

General Chou wears a blue denim suit which suggests traditional Chinese garb and at the same time looks like the dress of any skilled worker. He has an open face, with wide-spaced, serious eyes. He talks English slowly. He defined to me the nature of the compromises on both sides on which China's wartime united front has been built. He admitted impatience with what he regarded as the slowness of domestic reform in China, but assured me that the united front would last certainly until Japan was defeated. When I asked him if he thought it would survive the strain of the old Kuomintang-Communist enmity after the war, he frankly was not willing to make predictions. However, he had undoubted respect for and faith in the selfless devotion of the Generalissimo to China. He was not so sure of some of her other leaders. He left me with the feeling that if all Chinese Communists are like himself, their movement is more a national and agrarian awakening than an international or proletarian conspiracy.

Another man who impressed me deeply was Dr. Chang Po-ling. He is an enormous man, with the grave, deliberate manner of a scholar but a fine, warm sense of humor. He is the head of Nankai, one of the leading schools of China, and also a member of the People's Political Council. Whether we talked of India, or the war, or American universities, he spoke with a background and a judgment which would be hard to equal in the United States.

There were two other men in Chungking who illustrated for me the new China not to be found in any of the books I had read about traditional Chinese life. One was Li Wei-kuo, private secretary to the Generalissimo. He is young, wise beyond his years, and able in the sense that a great leader needs ability in his secretaries. The other was General J. L. Huang, Secretary General of the Officers' Moral

Endeavor Association. The general is as big and robust as his laugh, which is very big. It would be easy to describe him as an exceptionally talented host and manager. One of his jobs is to organize the hostels in which American fliers live in China, and he does it superbly. But underneath his jovial manner and his social skills, I found a thoughtful, patient, untiring fighter for China's victory and a better world.

China has no lack of good men for the top jobs in Chungking. But no matter how high the standard they set, the Soong family is in a class by itself in Chinese life. Three brothers and three sisters, all trained by Methodist missionaries and in American colleges, have given China an aristocracy of talent, political skill, great wealth, and unswerving devotion to the cause of the young republic. They make up one of the most remarkable families in the world.

I had known T. V. Soong in Washington. He is China's Foreign Minister, and one of the great statesmen of the United Nations. His three sisters I met in China. One is the wife of the Generalissimo. Another is the wife of H. H. Kung, who runs China's finances. The third is the widow of Dr. Sun Yat-sen, founder of the Chinese Republic.

At the dinner party given for me by Dr. Kung, served on the lawn, I was placed at the head table between Madame Sun and Madame Chiang. The conversation was lively, and I had a great time. Both ladies speak excellent English and are full of information and wit.

When the dinner was over, Madame Chiang took me by the arm. "I want you to meet my other sister. She has

neuralgia and couldn't come outdoors for the party." In-
doors, we found Madame Kung with her arm in a sling,
eager to hear about America, where she had lived as a girl.
The three of us talked and had such a good time we forgot
about the hour and the people outdoors.

About eleven o'clock, Dr. Kung came in and gently
scolded Madame Chiang and me for our failure to return
to the party, which by then had broken up. Then he sat
down, and the four of us set out to solve the problems of the
universe.

We talked about the revolution of ideas that is sweeping
the East—a subject that came up wherever I went—of India
and Nehru, of China and Chiang, of the overpowering
surge toward freedom of Asia's hundreds of millions, of
their demands for education and better living and, above
all, for the right to their own governments, independent of
the West.

To me, it was fascinating. All three of them knew their
facts. All three held strong opinions and each contributed
much to the conversation, especially Madame Chiang.
Finally, just before we were to leave, Madame Chiang said
to Dr. and Madame Kung: "Last night at dinner Mr.
Willkie suggested that I should go to America on a good-
will tour." The Kungs looked at me as if questioning. I
said: "That is correct, and I know I am right in suggesting
it."

Then Dr. Kung spoke, seriously. "Mr. Willkie, do you
really mean that, and, if so, why?"

I said to him, "Dr. Kung, you know from our conversation how strongly I believe that it is vital for my fellow countrymen to understand the problems of Asia and the viewpoint of its people, how sure I am that the future peace of the world probably lies in a just solution of the problems of the Orient after the war.

"Someone from this section with brains and persuasiveness and moral force must help educate us about China and India and their peoples. Madame would be the perfect ambassador. Her great ability—and I know she will excuse me for speaking so personally—her great devotion to China, are well known in the United States. She would find herself not only beloved, but immensely effective. We would listen to her as to no one else. With wit and charm, a generous and understanding heart, a gracious and beautiful manner and appearance, and a burning conviction, she is just what we need as a visitor."

She has now come to America, and ever since her moving address to Congress and her charming but pointed reminder to the President that the Lord helps those who help themselves America has applauded her gallantry and her cause.

Brigadier General Claire L. Chennault, commander of the China Air Task Force of the United States Army Air Forces, is a hard man to forget once you have talked with him. He is tall, swarthy, lean, and rangy, and there is something hard about his jaw and his eyes which contrasts curiously with his Louisiana drawl. He first went to China as an individual fighter and aerial strategist, to help train the Chinese air force. Later he organized the American Volunteer Group which covered itself with glory both in China and in Burma. He is in the Army now, and the Army is lucky to have him.

The story is now well known of what he and his men have done. They have shot down Japanese planes in combat with a loss ratio ranging from twelve to one to twenty to one. When I was in Chungking, the Chinese records showed his forces to have won more than seventy consecutive air battles against the Japanese without a single loss, in spite of the fact that the Americans were outnumbered in each battle. According to Colonel Meriam C. Cooper, his chief of staff, who came to lunch with me in Chungking one day and told me stories his commander would have blushed to hear, the general combines orthodox strategy in the air with fantastically unorthodox tactics, and the result is something the Japanese have clearly shown they do not like. And Major Kight, our own pilot, told me that General Chennault's system of information about weather, aerial operating conditions, and geography, in view of the facilities he had, was absolutely amazing. For there are no well-established meteorological stations in China to give information to aviators. General Chennault's men depend largely on information relayed over large areas by Chinese couriers and the grapevine route.

I learned for myself that General Chennault has no rival in popularity among the Chinese. A schoolteacher in Chengtu told me without a second's hesitation, when I asked who was the American best known and most liked by her students, "General Chennault." I also heard him discussed at length by the most important leaders of China, and always with enormous respect and affection.

I had several engagements to meet and talk with General Chennault, but each time they failed to come off. Finally, I flew out to his headquarters near Chungking in order to see him. When I found him on his own airfield, standing against a line of his P40 fighter planes, each of them painted to look like a giant shark, I understood why he found it hard to keep an engagement in Chungking.

He was running, by direct and personal command, one of the busiest and most exciting bases I have ever seen. His assignment includes defense not only of the sky over Chungking and Kunming, capital of Yünnan province, but also defense of the all-important air route over Burma from India. In addition to this, he has taken on a side job of bombing the Japanese in Canton, in Hong Kong, as far north as the Kailan mines near the Great Wall in the north of China. His air-raid detection service was one of the most ingenious and effective I have ever heard of. His men, nearly all of them southerners and a frightening number of them from Texas, swore by him and performed miracles for him.

I was shocked at only one thing I saw: the paucity of the material he had to work with. What he had done became even more incredible when one saw the limited force under his command. General Chennault belongs in the great tradition of American fighting men, and the fliers who serve under him deserve the best that we can give them and as much of it as we can give them.

What he asks for is amazingly little; and what we

have sent him falls far short of even that little. General Chennault speaks quietly but with great conviction of what could be done to harass the Japanese in China, to cut their supply lines through the China Sea, to give help to the great Chinese armies which could move forward across the plains of eastern China if they had an air cover of any sort. He told me that a limited air offensive in China could be maintained by transporting gasoline, oil, spare parts, and replacements over the Himalayas by the present air route.

He has a sense of bafflement at the failure of officials back home to see what to him is so clear.

For an offensive here would have more than military consequences. It would give new confidence to the Chinese armies, and it would give heart to the Chinese people. I came home from China convinced that we must avoid at all costs giving the Chinese the idea that we are going to disregard them for another year and concentrate our fighting in other theaters of war. Regardless of what this might do to Chinese resistance, it would complicate a morale problem already made dangerous by inflation, and it would imperil all our chances of a solid basis of understanding with China on which to build the peace and the postwar world.

I was conscious every day I was in China of the fact that China has been at war with Japan for more than five long years. I saw it in the incredible caves dug into the hills of Chungking, where the entire population of the city takes refuge when the Japanese bombing planes come over the city. I saw it in the skill and fortitude with which again and again the Chinese emerged from those caves, after the raids were over, to rebuild their devastated city and continue fighting back.

I did not see it, but heard about it, in the amazing tales which can be double-checked and riveted with proof in Chungking of the heroic civilian resistance which goes-on behind the Japanese lines in China. While I was in Chungking, footsore but happy Englishmen and Americans were still arriving from the Japanese-conquered cities of Shanghai, Hong Kong, and Peking. They had been passed on across half a continent from band to band of guerrilla fighters, Chinese who formed a living chain of resistance deep into Japanese territory. All the farmers of China are showing by daily acts of heroism their stake in freedom and their eagerness to fight for it.

I also saw evidence that China had been fighting a long time in a Chinese military organization, which was news to me and, I found later, to many Chinese themselves. The picture many Americans still have of a Chinese army as a band of professional ruffians whose generals are experts at dickering with the enemy was probably never anything more than a caricature of military affairs in a disunited, technically backward country. Today, it is not even a caricature. Military China is united; its leaders are trained and able generals; its new armies are tough, fighting organizations of men who know both what they are fighting for and how to fight for it, even though they markedly lack any quantity of modern fighting equipment. In China, just as in Russia, this is truly a people's war. Even the sons of those of high estate enlist as privates in the army, an unthinkable act in China a generation ago, when service in the army was for hired and ignorant mercenaries.

I stood one afternoon outside Chengtu on a narrow bridge across a muddy but fast-running river. In front of me smoke rose in a heavy, blinding wall along the bank of the river. Through it could be seen flashes of machine-gun fire. Mortars were pounding in the fields behind me. The river was full of young Chinese, swimming desperately against the heavy current, some carrying rifles above their heads, others carrying ropes attached to a pontoon bridge.

They took the bridge across the river, although at one time when the current caught it full I would have given heavy odds that they could never make it. Then suddenly hundreds of other soldiers rose from the fields behind me, their helmets and uniforms so carefully camouflaged that I had never seen them. They ran across the pontoon bridge, scrambled up the other bank, and deployed for an attack on a village perhaps a mile away.

They took the village, but not until they had cut their way through barbed wire, threaded through a mine field which lifted heavy columns of smoke into the air whenever a mine was touched off, and finally wormed their way on their bellies across an open field with no cover. They entered the village with full equipment, hot and tired and dirty and proud of their newly won knowledge of how to carry out a complicated operation in the field.

For this had been a maneuver, a training exercise, at the Chengtu Military Academy, the largest in China. It had been organized by a Chinese graduate of West Point, who stood beside me and explained the rules of the exercise while it was going on. At least a large part of the 10,000 students regularly in training there to become officers in the new Chinese Army had taken part in it. It had been an exciting show, as professional as any similar exercise anywhere in the world. For me, what I saw that afternoon and was to see again and again in China marked the end of an era—the era in which 400,000,000 Chinese could be kicked around by any army, Japanese or English or American, for that matter.

I saw evidence of the fact that China had been fighting for five years again the next day at the Air Corps training school also at Chengtu. Here I saw hundreds of Chinese cadets—the men of whom it was thought charitable to say only a few years ago that they were "not a fighting race"—slash and hammer each other with heavy sticks, in the Japanese style, shouting and screaming while they belabored each other, in the toughest personal combat training I have ever watched. Here, too, I saw Chinese Boy Scouts, some as young as eight years old, going through the full discipline and training of army life in preparation for careers as professional soldiers.

I told "Holly" Tong that I wanted to see the Chinese front at some sector. At first, it seemed impossible. It was only later that I learned that the Generalissimo's solicitude for my safety while I was in China had had to be overcome, and that "Holly" had required time to accomplish this. Finally a trip was arranged, and although we were to find less physical danger than we expected, we were to have another lesson in how much the Chinese have learned in their five years of all-out war.

We flew to Sian, one of the ancient capitals of China, near the great bend in the Yellow River where it starts to flow eastward to the sea. We drove miles outside the city and climbed, by the light of Chinese lanterns strung along a mountain path, up to another military academy, this one the school where Chiang Kai-shek was living just before his famous kidnaping at Sian in 1936. That evening we set out for the front, incongruously enough, in luxurious sleeping cars on one of the few railroads left in free China.

We left the train at dawn the next morning, and rode another fifteen miles on handcars. A few miles from the river, which at this sector is the front, one of the generals with us decided we looked too much like sitting pigeons to the Japanese across the river, and we took to our own legs, walking the last few miles along a road cut, like a trench, deep into the red loam of central China.

The front turned out to be a village surrounded by a network of trenches. The river is 1200 yards across at this point, but through artillery telescopes in the forward observation posts we could look down the muzzles of Japanese guns pointed at us and see the Japanese soldiers in their own encampments. It was quiet while we were there, but it was clear that it was not always quiet; in fact, there had been a bombardment just before our arrival.

It was at this front that I met Captain Chiang Wei-kao, son of the Generalissimo by an earlier marriage. Captain Chiang, who speaks perfect English, showed us in a long day the reasons why the Japanese had been unable to push across the river here, where there is a gap in the mountains, the traditional invasion route of south China.

We saw artillery and infantry and armored cars and fortresses built into the hills so deep that Japanese would have to blast them out. We saw a review of the 208th Division, one of the Generalissimo's crack units, well trained, well uniformed, and equipped with good, modern weapons. I talked to these soldiers, some 9000 of them standing in the blazing sun. They looked up at the little wooden platform which had been given me to stand on, and it seemed to me that not one man wavered in his attention until I had finished, although I was speaking in English. When what I said had been translated, they cheered so loudly that the Japanese must have heard them and wondered what the excitement was all about.

Back in our train again, where we sat down to dinner, Captain Chiang demonstrated conclusively to me that the front I had just seen was more than a showplace. He walked into the dining car with his arms full of Japanese cavalry swords, as presents for my party, and excellent French wine. Both had been captured by raiding parties which crossed the river at night, struck swiftly behind the Japanese lines, and returned with booty like this and more important trophies, including prisoners and military plans. Sometimes, Captain Chiang told me, such raiding parties stay for weeks inside the enemy lines, cutting communications and organizing sabotage, before returning to their own headquarters on the west bank of the river.

9

Some Notes on Chinese Inflation

I LEFT CHINA somewhat baffled by its present economic
and inflationary problems. Obviously its inflation
would have long since been disastrous, measured in terms
of a money economy, and yet financial disaster never quite
comes to China. One has a feeling, however, that it's just
around the proverbial corner and has been for a long while.

Price indices in China are not everything an American
banker would want before deciding on an answer to an inflationary situation. Prices were markedly different in the several cities we visited. And it was made clear to me every day
that enormous numbers of Chinese live largely outside the
money economy of their country and are independent of
prices, except for scant clothing needs and a few essential
manufactured goods. But even admitting these qualifica-
tions, the signs of inflation around us were disturbing in the
extreme to an American.

In Chungking, I was told, wholesale prices have risen to

at least fifty times their prewar level. Retail prices are in many cases sixty times higher than they were. During the few months before my arrival in October, the rate of increase was about ten per cent a month. For whole groups of the population, and especially those who live on fixed incomes, this has meant that many articles formerly consumed are now all but unattainable.

In Chengtu, two young women teachers helped me out with interpreting on a busy day. They were both educated women, who spoke good English. They were obviously the best type of citizen in a young republic still desperately short of trained personnel. They told me that living costs had risen so sharply, however, that they could no longer afford to eat as well as, for example, the most humble freight-carrying coolies, who live not on fixed salaries but on wages which have also reflected the inflation.

In the same city, where I discussed the problems of Chinese education with the heads of most of China's great universities, I found that the universities' income had in many cases held steady or actually increased. United China Relief had helped enormously to keep university budgets close to their prewar figures. But against prices that have multiplied fifty times, the value of American currency in terms of Chinese money has risen only about three times. As a result, the universities face the same crisis now as their teachers and their students.

There are several reasons, as I saw it, for this inflation. The first is that China has been forced to finance the war by the issue of paper money. In 1942, only about one quarter of the expenses of the government were covered by taxation. New government monopolies, which now include salt, sugar, matches, tobacco, tea, and wine, have helped to increase revenue, but not nearly enough. There is almost no public saving in China, to absorb government loans. So, to continue the war, the government has been forced to continue to use the printing presses. Much of the cargo flown over the Himalayas, I learned from pilots on the run, is paper money to meet the steadily growing costs of fighting the war.

This is in part due to the failure of the government itself to adopt a sound fiscal policy, a system of monetary and price control, and a method of adequate income and other taxation that would drain off the increased profits and incomes among some groups created by the inflation itself. The government has also failed rigidly to enforce its directives against speculation in basic commodities. Some of the independent editors in China insisted to me that speculation was indulged in even by government officials themselves. Everyone told me that the Generalissimo was using his utmost efforts to stamp out the irregularities, to bring about some financial order, and to eliminate any corrupt elements. But the Generalissimo is not a man schooled in finance or the intricacies of a fiscal policy. His training and his bent are in other directions.

Another reason for this inflationary development is the acute shortage of goods in free China, which is in part created by our own failure to send goods to China, and in part by the Japanese conquest of most of China's earlier-developed industrial regions and the cutting off of China's access to the world except through Russia and over the Himalayas. China needs both raw materials and certain essential machinery for any large-scale production inside the limits of free China. Both of these are now extremely difficult to secure.

Judging by what I saw myself, the Chinese have done miracles to meet this problem, but miracles have not been enough. Dr. Wong Wen-hao, Minister of Economics, showed me on one exciting day in Chungking a cotton mill which had been moved to Szechwan from Honan province, and a paper mill which had been moved from Shanghai in 1938. In all, he told me, the government had succeeded in transporting close to 120,000 tons of equipment inland, most of it concentrated in the iron and steel and spinning and weaving industries.

Both mills were fair-sized, efficient-looking plants. The paper mill, by the way, was about to begin the manufacture of bank-note paper. Its present capacity is from five to nine tons of such paper a day, Dr. Wong told me, and the comparison of that figure with the needs of 100,000,000 people living in free China was illustration enough of the grave problem which China faces in trying to build a new economic base in the middle of a war.

The Chinese Industrial Co-operatives, which I saw in Lanchow, have helped to meet the problem, but they have had difficulties growing out of disagreement over who should control them. It is the belief of those who operate them that there are certain financial and industrial forces in China seeking to destroy them. But they have in the Generalissimo, with whom I discussed their problems in detail, a firm and steadfast friend. It would be hard for them in any case to meet in the immediate future the demands of the war on production without a heavy-industry base, and without anything like adequate transport. Free China has left something less than a thousand miles of railroad. The Russian highway, as I pointed out before, is the only open land route over which exports and imports can move, and the capacity of the Himalaya air route and of the smuggling routes through the Japanese lines is strictly limited.

This is the problem, then, and the best minds I found in China, both Chinese and foreign, were looking for a solution. What this solution will be I could not say without a great deal more study of the problem. But I am sure that one of its chief features must be a loosening of the tight controls over Chinese economic life and of hereditary property and a mobilization of the enormous human resources of the country for the production of goods and services on a far larger scale than at present.

Members of the government were inclined, I thought, to take a far less serious view of inflation than many Americans I talked with. They pointed out to me that only the Chinese middle class has fixed incomes so low that their living standard is jeopardized by inflation, and that this middle class consists of a very small number of people. They claimed that coolies, manual labor in general, and many farmers who had no fixed income but were getting high prices for their products were actually profiting from the inflation.

There is this to be said for that viewpoint: that one who

attempts to measure the inflationary problems of China in the light of similar problems in an economy such as ours may well come to some shockingly erroneous conclusions. One of the best students of Chinese economics I met estimated to me that eighty per cent of the Chinese people grow their own food and have little need for money. Their money purchasing power has always been almost insignificant.

But this argument cannot be carried too far. Although it made the present situation seem less desperate, it held out little hope for the future. Governor Chang Chun of Szechwan province, one of the most skilled and thoughtful administrators I met in China, told me that seventy per cent of the men actually raising crops in his province were either full or part tenants of the land they tilled. These men paid their rents, he said, in kind and not in cash, and therefore any rise in the price of food would benefit them only slightly, while a corresponding rise in the cost of even the few things they were required to buy might well eat up the thin margin of subsistence on which most Chinese farmers live.

Most important of all, however, was the ugly fact that Chinese economy is still poor, desperately poor. It must have, to finance the war or to finance the reconstruction which must follow the war, immensely greater productive organization of its natural resources. No one can doubt this fact who has seen the resources, both in human and raw-material terms, and who has sensed the deep, driving determination of the Chinese people themselves to mobilize these resources.

A greater flow of goods and services, scaled up to what

China is capable of in technical terms, would be probably the best solution, it seemed to me, for inflation in China. It is up to the Chinese people to decide how they want to organize and finance that greater flow and production of goods and services. More widespread ownership of the land than I found anywhere in China would help. So would a greater degree of decentralization of financial control, I thought, after I had talked with young Chinese bankers and factory managers in Sian and Lanchow. The government will inevitably play an important part; it seemed to me it might be wise to cut the people in on it to a larger extent. But these are questions for the Chinese to decide.

Meanwhile there is much that America can do to help. First, I am convinced, we must make our friendship for the Chinese, who are fighting on our side, more real and tangible. We must send them, through Russia, over the Himalayas, or by reconquering Burma, or by all three routes, machines and airplanes and ammunition and the raw materials they need.

But we must also think out this alliance for ourselves, and decide what it really means to us. We must decide whether or not we can ever find a better ally in eastern Asia than the Chinese, and if the answer is negative, as I predict it will be, then we must be prepared to fulfill the obligations of an ally. These obligations will include economic co-operation and present military help. But they also include the obligation to understand the Chinese and their problems. Chinese faith in noble phrases and protestations is wearing a little thin.

10

Our Reservoir of Good Will

W E LEFT CHENGTU on October 9, traveled almost a thousand miles in China, crossed the vast expanse of the Gobi and the Mongolian Republic, crossed thousands of miles of Siberia, crossed the Bering Sea, the full length of Alaska and the full width of Canada, and arrived in the United States on October 13. We had gained a day by crossing the international date line.

When you fly around the world in forty-nine days, you learn that the world has become small not only on the map, but also in the minds of men. All around the world, there are some ideas which millions and millions of men hold in common, almost as much as if they lived in the same town. One of these ideas, and one which I can report without hesitation, has tremendous significance for us in America; it is the mixture of respect and hope with which the world looks to this country.

Whether I was talking to a resident of Belém or Natal in

Brazil, or one toting his burden on his head in Nigeria, or a prime minister or a king in Egypt, or a veiled woman in ancient Bagdad, or a shah or a weaver of carpets in legendary Persia, now known as Iran, or a follower of Ataturk in those streets of Ankara which look so like the streets of our Middle Western cities, or to a strong-limbed, resolute factory worker in Russia, or to Stalin himself, or the enchanting wife of the great Generalissimo of China, or a Chinese soldier at the front, or a fur-capped hunter on the edge of the trackless forests of Siberia—whether I was talking to any of these people, or to any others, I found that they all have one common bond, and that is their deep friendship for the United States.

They, each and every one, turn to the United States with a friendliness that is often akin to genuine affection. I came home certain of one clear and significant fact: that there exists in the world today a gigantic reservoir of good will toward us, the American people.

Many things have created this enormous reservoir. At the top of the list go the hospitals, schools, and colleges which Americans—missionaries, teachers, and doctors—have founded in the far corners of the world. Many of the new leaders of old countries—men who are today running Iraq or Turkey or China—have studied under American teachers whose only interest has been to spread knowledge. Now, in our time of crisis, we owe a great debt to these men and women who have made friends for us.

Good will has also been stored up for us, like credit in a bank account, by those Americans who have pioneered in the opening of new roads, new airways, new shipping lines. Because of them, the peoples of the world think of us as a people who move goods, and ideas, and move them fast. They like us for this, and they respect us.

Our motion pictures have played an important role in building up this reservoir of friendliness. They are shown all over the world. People of every country can see with their own eyes what we look like, can hear our voices. From Natal to Chungking I was plied with questions about American motion-picture stars—questions asked eagerly by shop-girls and those who served me coffee, and just as eagerly by the wives of prime ministers and kings.

There are still other reasons for our reserve of good will abroad. The people of every land, whether industrialized or not, admire the aspirations and accomplishments of American labor, which they have heard about, and which they long to emulate. Also they are impressed by American methods of agriculture, business, and industry. In nearly every country I went to, there is some great dam or irrigation project, some harbor or factory, which has been built by Americans. People like our works, I found, not only because they help to make life easier and richer, but also because we have shown that American business enterprise does not necessarily lead to attempts at political control.

I found this dread of foreign control everywhere. The fact that we are not associated with it in men's minds has caused people to go much farther in their approval of us than I had dared to imagine. I was amazed to discover how keenly the world is aware of the fact that we do not seek—

anywhere, in any region—to impose our rule upon others or to exact special privileges.

All the people of the earth know that we have no sinister designs upon them, that even when we have in the past withdrawn from international affairs into a false self-sufficiency, it was without sinister purpose. And they know that, now we are in this war, we are not fighting for profit, or loot, or territory, or mandatory power over the lives or the governments of other people. That, I think, is the single most important reason for the existence of our reservoir of good will around the world.

Everywhere I went around the world, and I mean literally everywhere, I found officers and men of the United States Army. Sometimes they were in very small units; in other places they filled enormous army camps which covered acres of some foreign country. In every situation in which I found them, they were adding to the good will foreign peoples hold toward America.

A striking example of this was the crew of our C-87 army plane. None of its officers or enlisted men had ever been abroad before except on a fighting assignment. They were not trained diplomats. Most of them spoke no foreign language. But everywhere we landed, they made friends for America. I shall remember for a long time the sight of the Shah of Iran, just after we had given him the first airplane ride of his life, shaking hands with Major Richard Kight, our pilot, and looking at him with what I can only describe as a mixture of admiration and envy.

I was proud of American soldiers everywhere I saw them.

I felt a confidence that our citizens' army, uninterested in entrenching themselves as professional army men, would automatically help to preserve the reservoir of good will which our generation inherits, and would at the same time find out, through firsthand experience, why this is America's war.

For, as I see it, the existence of this reservoir is the biggest political fact of our time. No other Western nation has such a reservoir. Ours must be used to unify the peoples of the earth in the human quest for freedom and justice. It must be maintained so that, with confidence, they may fight and work with us against the gigantic evil forces that are seeking to destroy all that we stand for, all that they hope for. The preservation of this reservoir of good will is a sacred responsibility, not alone toward the aspiring peoples of the earth, but toward our own sons who are fighting this battle on every continent. For the water in this reservoir is the clean, invigorating water of freedom.

Neither Hitler nor Mussolini nor Hirohito, with their propaganda or by their arms, can take from us the unifying force of this good will—and there is no other such unifying force in the world—or divide us among ourselves or from our allies, as long as we do not make a mockery of our protestations of the ideals for which we have proclaimed we fight. A policy of expediency will prove inexpedient. For it will lose us the invaluable spiritual and practical assets that come from the faith of the people of the world in both our ideals and our methods.

If we permit ourselves to become involved in the machinations of Old World intrigue and religious, nationalistic and racial blocs, we will find ourselves amateurs indeed. If we stand true to our basic principles, then we shall find ourselves professionals of the kind of world toward which men in every part of it are aspiring.

11

What We Are Fighting For

IT HAS BECOME BANAL to say that this war is a revolution, in men's thinking, in their way of living, all over the world. It is not banal to see that revolution taking place, and that is what I saw. It is exciting and a little frightening. It is exciting because it is fresh proof of the enormous power within human beings to change their environment, to fight for freedom with an instinctive, awakened confidence that with freedom they can achieve anything. It is frightening because the different peoples of the United Nations, let alone their leaders, have by no means reached common agreement as to what they are fighting for, the ideas with which we must arm our fighting men.

For, however important the role of bayonets and guns may have been in the development of mankind, the role of ideas has been vastly more important—and, in the long run, more conclusive. In historical times, at any rate, men have not often fought merely for the joy of killing each other.

They have fought for a purpose. Sometimes that purpose has not been very inspiring. Sometimes it has been quite selfish. But a war won without a purpose is a war won without victory.

A most outstanding example of a war fought with a purpose was our own American Revolution. We did not fight the Revolution because we hated Englishmen and wanted to kill them, but because we loved freedom and wanted to establish it. I think it is fair to say, in the light of what that freedom has meant to the world, that the victory won at Yorktown was the greatest victory ever won by force of arms. But this was not because our army was large and formidable. It was because our purpose was so clear, so lofty, and so well defined.

Unhappily this cannot be said of the war of 1914-18. It has become almost a historical truism that that was a war without victory. Of course, it is true that, while we were engaged in it, we thought, or said, that we were fighting for a high purpose. Woodrow Wilson, our Commander in Chief, stated our purpose in eloquent terms. We were fighting to make the world safe for democracy—to make it safe, not just with a slogan, but by accepting a set of principles known as the Fourteen Points, and by setting up a full-fledged international structure to be known as the League of Nations. That was a high purpose, surely. But when the time came to execute it in a peace treaty, a fatal flaw was discovered. We found that we and our allies were not really agreed upon that purpose. On the one hand, some of our allies had entangled themselves in secret treaties; and they were more in-tent upon carrying out those treaties, and upon pursuing traditional power diplomacy, than upon opening up the new vista that Mr. Wilson had sought to define. And, on the other hand, we ourselves were not so deeply dedicated to our declared purposes as we had led the world to believe. The net result was the abandonment of most of the purposes for which the war had supposedly been fought. Because those purposes were abandoned, that war was denounced by our generation as an enormous and futile slaughter. Millions had lost their lives. But no new idea, no new goal, rose from the ashes of their sacrifice.

Now I think that these considerations lead us inescapably to one conclusion. I think we must conclude that, generally speaking, nothing of importance can be won in peace which has not already been won in the war itself. I say nothing of importance. It is quite true, of course, that many details must be worked out at the peace table and at conferences succeeding the peace table—details which cannot be judiciously worked out under the pressure of war. We —we and our allies, of course—cannot, for instance, stop fighting the Japanese to make a detailed plan of what we intend to do about Burma when victory is won. Nor can we relent in our pressure against Hitler to decide the detailed future of Poland now.

What we must win now, during the war, are the principles. We must know what our line of solution will be. Again, let me use the American Revolution as an example. When we fought that war, we had no inkling of the actual structure of the United States of America. No one had ever heard of the Constitution. The federal system, the three branches of government, the brilliant bicameral compromise by which the small states were induced to come into the Union—all these innovations lay as yet in the future, nourished only by the brains of a few great political thinkers—who, themselves, were not entirely clear. And yet the basic principles of that great political structure that was to become the United States of America were, surely, contained in the Declaration of Independence, in the songs and speeches of that day, in after-dinner discussions and private arguments around soldiers' campfires and everywhere along the Atlantic Coast. Even though the great states of Massachusetts and Virginia were held together by the vaguest pronouncements and the flimsiest of political contraptions (the Continental Congress), their citizens were in substantial agreement as to the cause they were fighting for and the goal they wished to achieve.

Had they not agreed during the war, Massachusetts and Virginia, surely, would have failed to agree concerning the principles of the peace. They won in the peace exactly what they won in the war—no more and no less. This truth, if it were not self-evident, could be proved by citing one calamity. The people of those states did fail to agree concerning the freedom or slavery of the Negro. The result was that there grew up around the enslaved Negro in the South an entirely different economy from that which grew up in the North. And this resulted in another, and far bloodier, war.

Can we not learn from this simple lesson, and from similar lessons of history, what our task is today? We must learn. We must know that we shall win in the future peace only what we are now winning in the war—no more and no less.

First, to determine what we want to win, it is clearly necessary to reach substantial agreement with our allies. Here, as in our own Revolution, agreement in detail is not necessary, or even desirable. But unless we are to repeat the unhappy history of the last war, agreement in principle must be won. Moreover, it must exist not just among the leaders of the allies. The basic agreement I am thinking of must be established among the allied peoples themselves. We must make sure that we are all fighting for essentially the same thing.

Now what does this mean? It means that every one of us has the obligation to speak out, to exchange ideas, freely and frankly, across the Pacific, across the Atlantic, and here at home. Unless the British people know the way we are thinking in America, and take it to heart, and unless we have a similar idea of what they are thinking in England and in the Commonwealth, there can be no hope of agreement. We must know what the people of Russia and China aim for and we must let them know our aims.

It is the utmost folly—it is just short of suicide—to take the position that citizens of any country should hold their tongues for fear of causing distress to the immediate and sometimes tortuous policies of their leaders.

We have been told, for example, that private citizens, particularly those not expert in military affairs or those un-connected with government, should refrain from making

suggestions about the conduct of the war—military, industrial, economic, or political. It is said that we must remain
silent and allow our leaders and the experts to solve these
problems unmolested.

This position threatens, I believe, to become a tight wall
which will keep the truth out and lock misrepresentation
and false security within. I reported to the American people
when I returned last fall that in many important respects
we were not doing a good job; that we were on the road to
winning the war, but that we ran a heavy risk of spending
far more in men and materials than we need to spend. That
report was based on facts. Such facts should not be censored.
They should be given to us all. For unless we recognize and
correct our mistakes, we may lose the friendship of half our
allies before the war is over and then lose the peace.

It is plain that to win this war we must make it our war,
the war of all of us. In order to do this we must all know as
much about it as possible, subject only to the needs of military security. A misdirected censorship will not accomplish
this.

France had a military leader by the name of Maginot.
When a farsighted citizen of France occasionally suggested
that perhaps conditions of modern warfare were such that
fortresses built underground would not be adequate against
airplanes and tanks, he was reminded that he should leave
such matters to the experts.

The record of this war to date is not such as to inspire
in us any sublime faith in the infallibility of our political,
military, and naval experts. Military experts, as well as our

leaders, must be constantly exposed to democracy's greatest driving power—the whiplash of public opinion, developed from honest, free discussion.

For instance, it was public criticism of the constant failures in North Africa at the time of Rommel's great victory that brought about a change of command there. When I was in Egypt, that new command stopped Rommel. It has since driven him three-quarters of the way across Africa. I think some of the credit for that victory should be chalked up to British public opinion.

People in the United States are apt to conclude that there is no such thing as public opinion or the operation of its power in countries under absolute forms of government. As a matter of fact, in every absolutely governed country I visited, the government had elaborate methods of determining what the people were thinking. Even Stalin has his form of "Gallup poll," and it is recorded that Napoleon at the height of his power, as he sat astride his white horse amid the smoldering ruins of Moscow, anxiously waited for his daily courier's report of what the mobs in Paris were thinking.

In every country I saw around the world, I found some kind of public opinion operating powerfully both on the course of the war and on the slowly emerging ideas of peace. In Bagdad I found it in the conversation in every coffeehouse, and there are a multitude of them. In Russia, it was expressed in great factory meetings and in the talk of Russians everywhere, who, however contrary it may seem to our notion of Soviet Russia, exchange ideas in private conversation almost as freely as we do. In China, newspapers, though not as unrestricted as ours, nevertheless with a sur‑ prising freedom reflect and lead public opinion. No man I talked to in China, whether he was the leader of the Com‑ munist party, a factory worker, a college professor, or a soldier seemed to have any hesitancy about expressing his views, and many of the views were in conflict with some of the policies of the government.

In every country I found worry and doubt in the hearts and minds of people behind the fighting fronts. They were searching for a common purpose. This was plain in the ques‑ tions they asked about America after the war, about Great Britain, and, when I was in China, about Russia. The whole world seemed to me in an eager, demanding, hungry, ambi‑ tious mood ready for incredible sacrifices if only they could see some hope that those sacrifices would prove worth while.

Europe in 1917 was probably in much the same mood. It is an inevitable corollary of blood and war weariness. Then, in 1917, Lenin gave the world one set of answers. A little later Wilson gave it another. Neither set of answers ever became blood-and-bone part of the war, but were superim‑ posed on it, in the various treaties of peace. So neither set of answers redeemed the war or made it anything more than a costly fight for power. It ended with an armistice, not a real peace.

I do not believe this war need be the same. There are now, during the war, common purposes in the minds of men living as far apart as the citizens of Great Britain and the Free Commonwealth of Nations, the Americans, the

Russians, and the Chinese. But we shall have to make articulate and real our common purposes.

The people must define their purposes during the war. I have quite deliberately tried to provoke discussion of those purposes among the peoples of the various countries of the world. For I live in a constant dread that this war may end before the people of the world have come to a common understanding of what they fight for and what they hope for after the war is over. I was a soldier in the last war and after that war was over, I saw our bright dreams disappear, our stirring slogans become the jests of the cynical, and all because the fighting peoples did not arrive at any common postwar purposes while they fought. It must be our resolve to see that that does not happen again.

Millions have already died in this war and many thousands more will go before it is over. Unless Britons and Canadians and Russians and Chinese and Americans and all our fighting allies, in the common co-operation of war, find the instrumentalities and the methods of co-operative effort after the war, we, the people, have failed our time and our generation.

Our leaders, jointly and singly, have expressed some of our common aspirations. One of the finest expressions came from Chiang Kai-shek in a message to the Western world, delivered through the *New York Herald Tribune* Forum on Current Events in New York City last November. He concluded:

China has no desire to replace Western imperialism in Asia with an Oriental imperialism or isolationism of its own or of

171

anyone else. We hold that we must advance from the narrow idea of exclusive alliances and regional blocs, which in the end make for bigger and better wars, to effective organization of world unity. Unless real world co-operation replaces both isolationism and imperialism of whatever form in the new interdependent world of free nations, there will be no lasting security for you or for us.

Add to this Stalin's statement of purpose, which I quoted earlier, a statement on November 6, 1942, on the occasion of the twenty-fifth anniversary of the October Revolution. It is a singularly explicit and exact statement:

Abolition of racial exclusiveness, equality of nations and integrity of their territories, liberation of enslaved nations and restoration of their sovereign rights, the right of every nation to arrange its affairs as it wishes, economic aid to nations that have suffered and assistance to them in attaining their material welfare, restoration of democratic liberties, the destruction of the Hitlerite regime.

Franklin Roosevelt has proclaimed the Four Freedoms and Winston Churchill, with Franklin Roosevelt, has announced to the world the pact of the Atlantic Charter.

The statement of Mr. Stalin and the Atlantic Charter seem to me to have a common fallacy. They forecast the re-creation of western Europe in its old divisions of small nations, each with its own individual political, economic, and military sovereignty. It was this outmoded system that caused millions in Europe to be captivated by Hitler's proposed new order. For even with Hitler tyranny they at least saw the hope of the creation of an area large enough so that the economics of the modern world could successfully function. They had come to realize through bitter experience that the restricted areas of trade imposed by the high walls of a multitude of individual nationalisms, with the consequent manipulations of power politics, made impoverishment and war inevitable.

The re-creation of the small countries of Europe as political units, *yes;* their re-creation as economic and military units, *no,* if we really hope to bring stabilization to western Europe both for its own benefit and for the peace and economic security of the world.

The statement of the Generalissimo, the declaration of Mr. Stalin, the provisions of the Atlantic Charter, and the enunciation of the Four Freedoms are nevertheless each and all signs of great progress and have aroused high hopes around the world.

If the performance, however, does not measure up to the professions or if individual aspirations of nations that make the performance impossible are interposed, the peoples of the world will turn to a corrosive cynicism that will destroy every chance of world order.

People everywhere, articulate and inarticulate people, are watching to see whether the leaders who proclaimed the principles of these documents really meant what they said.

Before I started on my trip, Mr. Winston Churchill had made two statements about the Atlantic Charter: (1) that its authors had "in mind primarily the restoration of the sovereignty, self-government, and national life of the states and nations of Europe now under the Nazi yoke"; and (2) that the provisions of the Charter did "not qualify in any way the various statements of policy which have been made from time to time about the development of constitutional government in India, Burma, or other parts of the British Empire." Practically every Prime Minister and Foreign Minister in every country I visited, as well as numberless people, asked me whether this meant that the Atlantic Charter was to be applied only to western Europe. I told them that I of course did not know what Mr. Churchill meant, but that obviously when Mr. Churchill said its authors had in mind primarily the countries of Europe, he did not necessarily exclude other countries. My auditors, without fail, brushed my answer aside with impatience as legalistic and trivial. That was one of the reasons why I was so greatly distressed when Mr. Churchill subsequently made his world-disturbing remark, "We mean to hold our own. I did not become His Majesty's first minister in order to preside over the liquidation of the British Empire." I have been cheered since, however, by discussion with many British now resident in the United States, by following the British press, and by an amazingly large and steadily continuing correspondence from people in England and all over the British Empire, to find that British public opinion on these matters is even ahead of opinion in the United States. The British have no doubt—and, so far as I can see, little regret—that the old imperialism must pass and that the principles of the British Free Commonwealth of Nations must be extended at a rapidly accelerating pace to all corners of the British Empire.

It is because also the performance of our leaders, in the light of their statements, is under test that our own policy in North Africa has seemed to me such a tragedy. It began when the President, in his proclamation of the triumphant entry of American forces into North Africa, instead of giving a candid reason for our entrance, gave as a reason the same age-old worn-out diplomatic formula that has never fooled anyone, certainly not Belgium and Holland when Hitler entered their territories and gave a similar reason: "In order to forestall an invasion of Africa by Germany and Italy, which if successful would constitute a direct threat to America across the comparatively narrow sea from western Africa, a powerful American force . . . is today landing on the Mediterranean and Atlantic coasts of the French colonies in Africa."

There followed the dealings with Darlan, the very symbol of all that free people had been taught to despise, on the ground of "temporary military expediency," an explanation which rendered it difficult to criticize without seeming to be disloyal to a fine military commander who had just accomplished, in conjunction with the British fleet, a brilliant piece of organizational strategy. The explanation, however, failed to satisfy many who did not believe that the soldier's mind conceived the deal, and felt they saw diplomacy once more, in devious ways, trading away the principles which we had proclaimed to the world.

The subsequent appointment of Peyrouton confirmed

their forebodings. Those of us who are troubled hope that something better than seems apparent will unfold. But even if that happens it is sure that had not America's reservoir of good will been so great, it could not have withstood this heavy draft on it. For the people of Russia and Great Britain and the conquered countries of Europe felt betrayed and baffled. Even in faraway China it was one more blow to a faith that had already been shocked by our arbitrary promise to return Indo-China to the French Empire. And at home it has done much to cause in the minds of those people who sincerely believed that we were fighting only a war of defense, a revival of the feeling that when the war is over we should withdraw again into our own borders.

Winston Churchill and Franklin Roosevelt are not the only leaders whose words and activities in the light of their proclamations are being watched. The failure of Mr. Stalin to announce to a worried world Russia's specific aspirations with reference to eastern Europe weighs the scales once more against the proclaimed purposes of leaders.

Neither the proclamations of leaders nor the opinion of the people of the world, however articulate, can accomplish anything unless we plan while we fight and unless we give our plans reality.

When the United Nations pact was announced, hundreds of millions of men and women in South America, in Africa, in Russia, in China, in the British Commonwealth, in the United States, in the conquered countries of Europe, perhaps even deep in Germany and Italy, thought they saw a vision of the nations signatory to that pact joining as partners in a common struggle to work together to free mankind. They thought that those nations would, during the war, sit in common council of strategy, of economic warfare, of planning for the future. For they knew that thus the war would be brought to a speedier end. They also knew that to learn to work together now would be the best insurance that the nations would learn to live together in the future.

More than a year has passed since the signing of the pact. Today the United Nations is a great symbol and a treaty of alliance. But we must face the fact that if hopeful billions of human beings are not to be disappointed, if the world of which we dream is to be achieved, even in part, then today, not tomorrow, the United Nations must become a common council, not only for the winning of the war but for the future welfare of mankind.

While we fight, we must develop a mechanism of working together that will survive after the fighting is over. Successful instruments of either national or international government are the result of growth. They cannot be created in a day. Nor is there much hope of their being created amid the reawakened nationalistic impulses, the self-seeking, the moral degenerations, and the economic and social dislocations that are always incident to a postwar period. They must be created now under the cementing force of common danger. They must be made workable and smooth-running, under the emery of day-to-day effort in the solution of common problems.

It is idle to talk about creating after the war is over a machinery for preventing economic warfare and promoting peace between nations, unless the parts of that machinery have been assembled under the unifying effort and common purpose of seeking to defeat the enemy. It is a mere dream to talk of full employment dependent upon international trade and development after the war, unless now while we fight together we learn to work together in accord, respect, and understanding. Can we, as some of our leaders have forecast, develop enormous trade relations with China and the Far East, unless today we are able to develop a joint military strategy with China? Can we hope to bring Russia, with its almost startling potentialities, within the orbit of a future co-ordinated economic world unless we have learned to work with her military strategists and her political leaders in common council?

What we need is a council today of the United Nations—a common council in which all plan together, not a council of a few, who direct or merely aid others, as they think wise. We must have a council of grand military strategy on which all nations that are bearing the brunt of the fighting are represented. Perhaps we might even learn something from the Chinese, who with so little have fought so well, so long. Or from the Russians who have recently seemed to know something about the art of war.

We must have a common council to amalgamate the economic strength of the United Nations toward total war production and to study jointly the possibilities of future economic co-operation.

And most important of all, as United Nations, we must formulate now the principles which will govern our actions

as we move step by step to the freeing of the conquered countries. And we must set up a joint machinery to deal with the
multiple problems that will accompany every forward step
of our victorious armies. Otherwise we will find ourselves
moving from one expediency to another, sowing the seeds
of future discontents—racial, religious, political—not alone
among the peoples we seek to free, but even among the
United Nations themselves. It is such discontents that have
wrecked the hopes of men of good will throughout the ages.

This Is a War of Liberation

THIS WAR that I saw going on all around the world is, in Mr. Stalin's phrase, a war of liberation. It is to liberate some nations from the Nazi or the Japanese Army, and to liberate others from the threat of those armies. On this much we are all agreed. Are we yet agreed that liberation means more than this? Specifically, are the thirty-one United Nations now fighting together agreed that our common job of liberation includes giving to *all* peoples freedom to govern themselves as soon as they are able, and the economic freedom on which all lasting self-government inevitably rests?

It is these two aspects of freedom, I believe, which form the touchstone of our good faith in this war. I believe we must include them both in our idea of the freedom we are fighting for. Otherwise, I am certain we shall not win the peace, and I am not sure we can win the war.

In Chungking, on October 7, 1942, I made a statement to

the Chinese and foreign press in which I tried to state some
of the conclusions I had reached on my trip around the
world. In part, this is what I said:

I have traveled through thirteen countries. I have seen king-
doms, soviets, republics, mandated areas, colonies, and depend-
encies. I have seen an almost bewildering variety of ways of living
and ways of ruling and of being ruled. But I have found certain
things common to all the countries I have visited and to all the
ordinary people in those countries with whom I have talked:

They all want the United Nations to win the war.

They all want a chance at the end of the war to live in liberty
and independence.

They all doubt, in varying degree, the readiness of the leading
democracies of the world to stand up and be counted for freedom
for others after the war is over. This doubt kills their enthusiastic
participation on our side.

Now, without the real support of these common people, the
winning of the war will be enormously difficult. The winning of
the peace will be nearly impossible. This war is not a simple,
technical problem for task forces. It is also a war for men's minds.
We must organize on our side not simply the sympathies but the
active, aggressive, offensive spirit of nearly three fourths of the
people of the world who live in South America, Africa, eastern
Europe, and Asia. We have not done this, and at present are not
doing this. We have got to do it. . . .

Men need more than arms with which to fight and win this
kind of war. They need enthusiasm for the future and a conviction that the flags they fight under are in bright, clean colors.
The truth is that we as a nation have not made up our minds
what kind of world we want to speak for when victory comes.

Especially here in Asia the common people feel that we have
asked them to join us for no better reason than that Japanese
rule would be even worse than Western imperialism. This is a

continent where the record of the Western democracies has been long and mixed, but where people—and remember there are a billion of them—are determined no longer to live under foreign control. Freedom and opportunity are the words which have modern magic for the people of Asia, and we have let the Japanese—the most cruel imperialists the modern world has known—steal these words from us and corrupt them to their own uses.

Most of the people in Asia have never known democracy. They may or may not want *our* type of democracy. Obviously all of them are not ready to have democracy handed to them next Tuesday on a silver platter. But they are determined to work out their own destiny under governments selected by themselves.

Even the name of the Atlantic Charter disturbs thoughtful men and women I have been talking to. Do all of those who signed it, these people ask, agree that it applies to the Pacific? We must answer this question with a clear and simple statement of where we stand. And we must begin to sweat over our common problem of translating such a statement into plans which will be concrete and meaningful to the lives of these millions of people who are our allies.

Some of the plans to which such a statement would lead are already clear, I deeply believe, to most Americans:

We believe this war must mean an end to the empire of nations over other nations. No foot of Chinese soil, for example, should be or can be ruled from now on except by the people who live on it. And we must say so *now*, not after the war.

We believe it is the world's job to find some system for helping colonial peoples who join the United Nations' cause to become free and independent nations. We must set up firm timetables under which they can work out and train governments of their own choosing, and we must establish ironclad guarantees, administered by all the United Nations jointly, that they shall not slip back into colonial status.

Some say these subjects should be hushed until victory is won.

Exactly the reverse is true. Sincere efforts to find progressive solutions now will bring strength to our cause. Remember, opponents of social change always urge delay because of some present crisis. After the war, the changes may be too little and too late.

We must develop between nations trade and trade routes strong enough to give all peoples the same vested interest in peace which we in America have had.

In the United States, we are being asked to give up temporarily our individual freedom and economic liberty in order to crush the Axis. We must recover this freedom and this liberty after the war. The way to make certain we do recover our traditional American way of life with a rising standard of living for all is to create a world in which all men everywhere can be free.

This statement caused a good deal of comment. Some of it was angry, but for the most part the reaction cheered me greatly. For it confirmed my feeling that the deep drift of public opinion, which works quietly but powerfully, has already moved ahead of many of our leaders on these questions and that it will, before long, push us into the open acknowledgment, before the world, of the beliefs we hold most firmly.

The temptation is great, in all of us, to limit the objectives of a war. Cynically, we may hope that the big words we have used will become smaller at the peace table, that we can avoid the costly and difficult readjustments which will be required to establish and defend real freedom for all peoples.

Many men and women I have talked with from Africa to Alaska asked me the question which has become almost a symbol all through Asia: what about India? Now I did not go to India. I do not propose to discuss that tangled question. But it has one aspect, in the East, which I should report. From Cairo on, it confronted me at every turn. The wisest man in China said to me: "When the aspiration of India for freedom was put aside to some future date, it was not Great Britain that suffered in public esteem in the Far East. It was the United States."

This wise man was not quarreling with British imperialism in India when he said this—a benevolent imperialism, if you like. He does not happen to believe in it, but he was not even talking about it. He was telling me that by our silence on India we have already drawn heavily on our reservoir of good will in the East. People of the East who would like to count on us are doubtful. They cannot ascertain from our attitude toward the problem of India what we are likely to feel at the end of the war about all the other hundreds of millions of Eastern peoples. They cannot tell from our vague and vacillating talk whether or not we really do stand for freedom, or what we mean by freedom.

In China, students who were refugees a thousand miles from their homes asked me if we were going to try to take back Shanghai after the war. In Beirut, Lebanese asked me if their relatives in Brooklyn—one third of all the Lebanese in the world live in the United States—would help to persuade the British and French occupying forces to leave Syria and the Lebanon after the war and let them run their own country.

In Africa, in the Middle East, throughout the Arab world, as well as in China and the whole Far East, freedom means the orderly but scheduled abolition of the colonial system. Whether we like it or not, this is true.

The British Commonwealth of Free Nations is the world's most spectacular example of such an orderly process. And the success of that great experiment should be immensely encouraging to the United Nations in working out the problems of self-government that lie ahead. For large sections of the world are still governed by the colonial system. Despite the Commonwealth, Great Britain still has numerous colonies, remnants of empire, with little or no self-rule, though the English people, millions of them, at home and throughout the Commonwealth, are working selflessly and with great skill toward reducing these remnants, toward extending the Commonwealth in place of the colonial system.

The English are by no means the only colonial rulers. The French still claim empire in Africa, in Indo-China, in South America, and in islands throughout the world. The Dutch still regard themselves as rulers of large parts of the East Indies and of territories in the West. The Portuguese, the Belgians, and other nations have colonial possessions. And we ourselves have not yet promised complete freedom to all the peoples in the West Indies for whom we have assumed responsibility. Furthermore, we have our domestic imperialisms.

But the world is awake, at last, to the knowledge that the rule of people by other peoples is not freedom, and not what we must fight to preserve.

There will be lots of tough problems ahead. And they will

differ in different mandates and different colonies. Not all the peoples of the world are ready for freedom, or can defend it, the day after tomorrow. But today they all want some date to work toward, some assurance that the date will be kept. For the future, they do not ask that we solve their problems for them. They are neither so foolish nor so fainthearted. They ask only for the chance to solve their own problems with economic as well as political co-operation. For the peoples of the world intend to be free not only for their political satisfaction, but also for their economic advancement.

13

Our Imperialisms at Home

I MENTIONED among the imperialisms of the world our own domestic imperialisms. This war has opened for us new horizons—new geographical horizons, new mental horizons. We have been a people devoted largely to home enterprise. We have become a people whose first interests are beyond the seas. The names of Russian, Burmese, Tunisian, or Chinese towns command primary attention in our newspapers. The most eagerly seized letters coming into our homes are from our young men in Australia, New Guinea, Guadalcanal, Ireland, or North Africa. Our interests go with their interests, and we may feel certain that when they have battled over the world, they will not return home as provincial Americans. Nor will they find us so. What does all this mean? It means that though we began to grow up with the earlier World War, we are only now changing completely from a young nation of domestic concerns to an adult nation of international interests and world outlook.

A true world outlook is incompatible with a foreign imperialism, no matter how high-minded the governing country. It is equally incompatible with the kind of imperialism which can develop inside any nation. Freedom is an indivisible word. If we want to enjoy it, and fight for it, we must be prepared to extend it to everyone, whether they are rich or poor, whether they agree with us or not, no matter what their race or the color of their skin. We cannot, with good conscience, expect the British to set up an orderly schedule for the liberation of India before we have decided for ourselves to make all who live in America free.

In this war we are allied with four hundred million people of China and we count as our friends three hundred million people of India. Fighting with us are the Filipinos and the natives of Java and the East Indies and of South Africa. Together, these peoples comprise almost half of the world's population. With none of them have the majority of Americans any ties of race. But we are learning in this war that it is not racial classifications nor ethnological considerations which bind men together; it is shared concepts and kindred objectives.

We are learning that the test of a people is their aim and not their color. Even Hitler's high racial wall has been breached by the recognition of a common purpose with those "honorary Aryans," the Japanese. We, too, have our natural allies. We must, now and hereafter, cast our lot as a nation with all those other peoples, whatever their race or color, who prize liberty as an innate right, both for themselves and for others. We must, now and hereafter, together with those peoples, reject the doctrine of imperialism which condemns the world to endless war.

Let me emphasize once more that race and color do not determine what people are allies and what people are enemies in this struggle. In the East, we have a plain example. Japan is our enemy because of her wanton and barbaric aggression upon weaker nations and because of the imperialistic doctrine by which she seeks to rule and enslave the world. Japan is our enemy because of the treacherous and unprovoked attacks by which she has launched each of her assaults in carrying forward her scheme of conquest.

China is our friend because like us she nourishes no dream of conquest and because she values liberty. She is our ally because, first among the nations, she resisted aggression and enslavement.

Here are two Oriental peoples. One is our enemy; one is our friend. Race and color have nothing to do with what we are fighting for today. Race and color do not determine at whose side we shall fight. These are things the white race is learning through this war. These are things we needed to learn.

Even our enemy, Japan, has been able to shock our racial complacency. She has rudely awakened us to the fact that the white race is not a select race and enjoys no superior rights in combat merely because of past progress and ascendancy. Whereas, a year and a half ago, we were generally contemptuous of Japan as a possible enemy, we now recognize that we have encountered a formidable foe, against whom we must marshal our full strength.

Our ally, China, has by the same token taught us a new and healthy humility. For we have seen her for more than five years, alone, with none of the equipment of modern warfare, defy that same formidable foe. And today her people still resist while we are still making ready to take our full share in the struggle. The moral atmosphere in which the white race lives is changing. It is changing not only in our attitude toward the people of the Far East. It is changing here at home.

It has been a long while since the United States had any imperialistic designs toward the outside world. But we have practiced within our own boundaries something that amounts to race imperialism. The attitude of the white citizens of this country toward the Negroes has undeniably had some of the unlovely characteristics of an alien imperialism—a smug racial superiority, a willingness to exploit an unprotected people. We have justified it by telling ourselves that its end is benevolent. And sometimes it has been. But so sometimes have been the ends of imperialism. And the moral atmosphere in which it has existed is identical with that in which men—well-meaning men—talk of "the white man's burden."

But that atmosphere is changing. Today it is becoming increasingly apparent to thoughtful Americans that we cannot fight the forces and ideas of imperialism abroad and maintain any form of imperialism at home. The war has done this to our thinking.

Emancipation came to the colored race in America as a war measure. It was an act of military necessity. Manifestly it would have come without war, in the slower process of humanitarian reform and social enlightenment. But it required a disastrous, internecine war to bring this question of human freedom to a crisis, and the process of striking the shackles from the slave was accomplished in a single hour. We are finding under the pressures of this present conflict that long-standing barriers and prejudices are breaking down. The defense of our democracy against the forces that threaten it from without has made some of its failures to function at home glaringly apparent.

Our very proclamations of what we are fighting for have rendered our own inequities self-evident. When we talk of freedom and opportunity for all nations, the mocking paradoxes in our own society become so clear they can no longer be ignored. If we want to talk about freedom, we must mean freedom for others as well as ourselves, and we must mean freedom for everyone inside our frontiers as well as outside. During a war, this is especially important.

The threat to racial and religious, even to political, minority groups springs in wartime from two things—an overzealous mass insistence upon general conformity to majority standards, and the revival under emotional strains of age-old racial and religious distrusts. Minorities then are apt to be charged with responsibility for the war itself, and all the dislocations and discomforts arising from it. They are jealously subjected to scrutiny to determine if they are the recipients of special advantages.

We are all familiar with the process by which, in a war psychology, the unusual is distrusted and anything unorthodox is associated by some people with enemy intriguing. Chauvinists are likely to spring up in any community. There is the instance in our War of 1812 of a young man arrested and held for espionage on the suspicious circumstances that "he carried a long whip and wore an unusual number of buttons on his pantaloons." When affairs go wrong the public, by ancient custom, demands a scapegoat, and the first place to seek one is from a minority.

All this would appear ridiculous in our modern age were it not for the examples of bigotry and persecution we see in countries once presumed to be enlightened, and, even more seriously, were it not for the fact that we are already witnessing a crawling, insidious anti-Semitism in our own country. It will be well to bear in mind continuously that we are fighting today against intolerance and oppression, and that we shall get them in abundance if we lose. If we allow them to develop at home while we are engaging the enemy abroad, we shall have immeasurably weakened our fighting arm.

Our nation is composed of no one race, faith, or cultural heritage. It is a grouping of some thirty peoples possessing varying religious concepts, philosophies, and historical backgrounds. They are linked together by their confidence in our democratic institutions as expressed in the Declaration of Independence and guaranteed by the Constitution for themselves and for their children.

The keystone of our union of states is freedom—freedom for the individual to worship as he chooses, to work as he chooses, and to live and rear his children as he chooses.

Liberty, if it is to be for all, must be protected by basic safeguards intended to give it the most general diffusion attainable, and none can expect privileges which encroach upon the rights of others. Despite the functionings of our mischievous bureaucracies, and our sometimes excessively enterprising legislatures, and—in deplorable but fortunately isolated instances—the flaring of mob law, we have obtained here in America, in the course of little more than a century and a half of experience and adjustment, the most reasonable expression of freedom that has yet existed in history.

Our success thus far as a nation is not because we have built great cities and big factories and cultivated vast areas, but because we have promoted this fundamental assurance of freedom upon which all our material development has depended, and have tolerated, and learned to use, our diversities.

We remain a relatively new nation. As recently as fifty years ago, more than half our mining and a third of our total manufacturing were carried on by immigrants. More than half of the farm population of some of our leading agricultural states was alien-born. In the formative period of the nation, between 1820 and 1890, more than 15,000,000 newcomers reached our shores, and a still greater number were yet to arrive in the twenty-four years preceding the outbreak of the last war. In other words, we have had two hundred years of reinvigorating immigration which has brought us new blood, new experiences, new ideas. Here was a vast assembly of minority groups which have gone

into the welding of a nation. We have created a strong nation because these new arrivals did not have the distrac-
tions, under our form of government, of continually opposing and battling one another, but entered as partners into
the general upbuilding and consolidation. The height of
our civilization, it seems to me, has been reached not by
our assembly lines, our inventions, or any of our great fac-
titious development, but by the ability of peoples of varying beliefs and of different racial extractions to live side by
side here in the United States with common understanding,
respect, and helpfulness.

If we want to see the opposite of this American system,
we have merely to look at the military despotism of Hitler
and the autocracy of Japan, and the fading dictatorship of
Fascist Italy. The story of Germany for the last ten years
has been one of racial and religious intolerance that provided a mask behind which a peace-professing dictator lured
the people first to minority persecution, then to war. This
intolerance gave the German nation the momentary
strength of complete regimentation. Actually, it has under-
mined and weakened the social structure so that when the
tide of war turns, collapse is likely to be sudden and complete.

It has always impressed me that, quite apart from any
reasons of humanitarianism or justice or any sentiment re-
garding the protection of the weak by the strong, it is only
common sense to safeguard jealously the rights of minorities. For minorities are rich assets of a democracy, assets
which no totalitarian government can afford. Dictatorships

must, of necessity, fear and suppress them. But within the tolerance of a democracy, minorities are the constant spring of new ideas, stimulating new thought and action, the constant source of new vigor.

To suppress minority thinking and minority expression would tend to freeze society and prevent progress. For the majority itself is stimulated by the existence of minority groups. The human mind requires contrary expressions against which to test itself.

For now more than ever, we must keep in the forefront of our minds the fact that whenever we take away the liberties of those whom we hate, we are opening the way to loss of liberty for those we love.

Our way of living together in America is a strong but delicate fabric. It is made up of many threads. It has been woven over many centuries by the patience and sacrifice of countless liberty-loving men and women. It serves as a cloak for the protection of poor and rich, of black and white, of Jew and gentile, of foreign- and native-born.

Let us not tear it asunder. For no man knows, once it is destroyed, where or when man will find its protective warmth again.

14

One World

IT WAS only a short time ago—less than a quarter of a century—that the allied nations gained an outstanding victory over the forces of conquest and aggression then led by imperial Germany.

But the peace that should have followed that war failed primarily because no joint objectives upon which it could be based had been arrived at in the minds of the people, and therefore no world peace was possible. The League of Nations was created full-blown; and men and women, having developed no joint purpose, except to defeat a common enemy, fell into capricious arguments about its structural form. Likewise, it failed because it was primarily an Anglo-French-American solution, retaining the old colonial imperialisms under new and fancy terms. It took inadequate account of the pressing needs of the Far East, nor did it sufficiently seek solution of the economic problems of the world. Its attempts to solve the world's problems were primarily political. But political internationalism without economic internationalism is a house built upon sand. For no nation can reach its fullest development alone.

Our own history furnishes, I believe, another clue to our failure. One of our most obvious weaknesses, in the light of what is going on today, is the lack of any continuity in our foreign policy. Neither major party can claim to have pursued a stable or consistent program of international co-operation even during the relatively brief period of the last forty-five years. Each has had its season of world outlook— sometimes an imperialistic one—and each its season of strict isolationism, the Congressional leadership of the party out of power usually, according to accepted American political practice, opposing the program of the party in power, whatever it might be.

For years many in both parties have recognized that if peace, economic prosperity, and liberty itself were to continue in this world, the nations of the world must find a method of economic stabilization and co-operative effort.

These aspirations at the end of the First World War, under the presidency of Woodrow Wilson, produced a program of international co-operation intended to safeguard all nations against military aggression, to protect racial minorities, and to give the oncoming generation some confidence that it could go about its affairs without a return of the disrupting and blighting scourge of war. Whatever we may think about the details of that program, it was definite, affirmative action for world peace. We cannot state positively just how effective it might have proved had the

United States extended to it support, influence, and active participation.

But we do know that we tried the opposite course and found it altogether futile. We entered into an era of strictest detachment from world affairs. Many of our public leaders, Democratic and Republican, went about the country proclaiming that we had been tricked into the last war, that our ideals had been betrayed, that never again should we allow ourselves to become entangled in world politics which would inevitably bring about another armed outbreak. We were blessed with natural barriers, they maintained, and need not concern ourselves with the complicated and unsavory affairs of an old world beyond our borders.

We shut ourselves away from world trade by excessive tariff barriers. We washed our hands of the continent of Europe and displayed no interest in its fate while Germany rearmed. We torpedoed the London Economic Conference when the European democracies, with France lagging in the rear, were just beginning to recover from the economic depression that had sapped their vitality, and when the instability of foreign exchange remained the principal obstacle to full revival. And in so doing, we sacrificed a magnificent opportunity for leadership in strengthening and rehabilitating the democratic nations, in fortifying them against assault by the forces of aggression which at that very moment were beginning to gather.

The responsibility for this does not attach solely to any political party. For neither major party stood consistently and conclusively before the American public as either the party of world outlook or the party of isolation. If we were to say that Republican leadership destroyed the League of Nations in 1920, we must add that it was Democratic leadership that broke up the London Economic Conference in 1933.

I was a believer in the League. Without, at this time, however, arguing either for or against the provisions of the League plans, I should like to point out the steps leading to its defeat here in the United States. For that fight furnishes a perfect example of the type of leadership we must avoid in this country if we are ever going to fulfill our responsibilities as a nation that believes in a free world, a just world, a world at peace.

President Wilson negotiated the peace proposals at Versailles, including the covenant of the League, without consultation with or the participation of the Republican leadership in the Senate. He monopolized the issue for the Democratic party and thereby strategically caused many Republicans—even international-minded Republicans—to take the opposite position. Upon his return the treaty and the covenant were submitted to the United States Senate for ratification. And there arose one of the most dramatic episodes in American history. I cannot here trace the details of that fight which resulted in rejection on the part of the United States of world leadership. It is important for us today, however, to remember the broad outlines of the picture.

First, as to the Senate group, the so-called "battalion of death," the "irreconcilables," or the "bitter-enders." Here

was a group that had no party complexion. In its leadership the name of the Democratic orator, James A. Reed,
occupies as conspicuous a position as that of the Republican, Borah. At the other extreme was the uncompromising war President, Woodrow Wilson, who insisted on the
treaty with every *i* dotted and every *t* crossed. Between them
were the reservationists, of various complexions and opinions, and of both Republican and Democratic affiliation.

We do not know today, and perhaps we never shall know,
whether the man who was then Republican leader of the
Senate, Henry Cabot Lodge, whose name we now asso-
ciate with the defeat of the League, truly wanted the League
adopted with safeguarding reservations or whether he em-
ployed the reservations to kill the League. Even his close
friends and members of his family have reported contrary
opinions on the subject.

But we do know that when this question passed from the
Senate to the two great political conventions of 1920, neither
of them stood altogether for, or altogether against, the
treaty as it had been brought home by the President. The
Democratic Convention in its platform did not oppose reservations. The Republican platform adopted a compromise
plank which was broad enough to accommodate the firm
supporters of the League in the Republican ranks. The anti-
League delegates found safe footing there too.

Both platforms were ambiguous; the parties had no consistent historical position about the co-operation of the
United States with other nations. The confusion was dou-
bled by the attitude of the Republican candidate, Warren

Harding, an amiable, pleasant man of no firm convictions. There was no doubt that Cox's position on the Democratic ticket was a fairly definite support of the Wilson treaty, though his party platform left open the possibility of reservations and many of the Democratic leaders were strongly in opposition. But no one was certain whether Harding was merely pulling his punches against the League or whether he intended to support it upon election, in a modified form. All that was clear was that he felt he had to make some opposition to the League since it had been made a political issue by the Democrats. In private conversation, he gave each man the answer he wanted. It was not until after the election returns were in that Harding spoke frankly of the League as "now deceased."

The election, ironically, had turned primarily on different questions. The great cause of America's co-operation with the world was put to the test of an election dominated by local issues through the fault of both parties. The Democratic party and its leaders unwisely sought to monopolize the international position and the Republican party equally unwisely allowed itself to be pushed strategically in the opposite direction. The time is approaching when we must once more determine whether America will assume its proper position in world affairs, and we must not let that determination be again decided by mere party strategy.

I am satisfied that the American people never deliberately and intentionally turned their backs on a program for international co-operation. Possibly they would have preferred changes in the precise Versailles covenant, but not complete aloofness from the efforts of other nations. They were betrayed by leaders without convictions who were thinking in terms of group vote catching and partisan advantage.

If our withdrawal from world affairs after the last war was a contributing factor to the present war and to the economic instability of the past twenty years—and it seems plain that it was—a withdrawal from the problems and responsibilities of the world after this war would be sheer disaster. Even our relative geographical isolation no longer exists.

At the end of the last war, not a single plane had flown across the Atlantic. Today that ocean is a mere ribbon, with airplanes making regular scheduled flights. The Pacific is only a slightly wider ribbon in the ocean of the air, and Europe and Asia are at our very doorstep.

America must choose one of three courses after this war: narrow nationalism, which inevitably means the ultimate loss of our own liberty; international imperialism, which means the sacrifice of some other nation's liberty; or the creation of a world in which there shall be an equality of opportunity for every race and every nation. I am convinced the American people will choose, by overwhelming majority, the last of these courses. To make this choice effective, we must win not only the war, but also the peace, and we must start winning it now.

To win this peace three things seem to me necessary— first, we must plan now for peace on a world basis; second, the world must be free, politically and economically, for nations and for men, that peace may exist in it; third,

America must play an active, constructive part in freeing it and keeping its peace.

When I say that peace must be planned on a world basis, I mean quite literally that it must embrace the earth. Continents and oceans are plainly only parts of a whole, seen, as I have seen them, from the air. England and America are parts. Russia and China, Egypt, Syria and Turkey, Iraq and Iran are also parts. And it is inescapable that there can be no peace for any part of the world unless the foundations of peace are made secure throughout all parts of the world.

This cannot be accomplished by mere declarations of our leaders, as in an Atlantic Charter. Its accomplishment depends primarily upon acceptance by the peoples of the world. For if the failure to reach international understanding after the last war taught us anything it taught us this: even if war leaders apparently agree upon generalized principles and slogans while the war is being fought, when they come to the peace table they make their own interpretations of their previous declarations. So unless today, while the war is being fought, the people of the United States and of Great Britain, of Russia and of China, and of all the other United Nations, fundamentally agree on their purposes, fine and idealistic expressions of hope such as those of the Atlantic Charter will live merely to mock us as have Mr. Wilson's Fourteen Points. The Four Freedoms will not be accomplished by the declarations of those momentarily in power. They will become real only if the people of the world forge them into actuality.

When I say that in order to have peace this world must

be free, I am only reporting that a great process has started which no man—certainly not Hitler—can stop. Men and women all over the world are on the march, physically, intellectually, and spiritually. After centuries of ignorant and dull compliance, hundreds of millions of people in eastern Europe and Asia have opened the books. Old fears no longer frighten them. They are no longer willing to be Eastern slaves for Western profits. They are beginning to know that men's welfare throughout the world is interdependent. They are resolved, as we must be, that there is no more place for imperialism within their own society than in the society of nations. The big house on the hill surrounded by mud huts has lost its awesome charm.

Our Western world and our presumed supremacy are now on trial. Our boasting and our big talk leave Asia cold. Men and women in Russia and China and in the Middle East are conscious now of their own potential strength. They are coming to know that many of the decisions about the future of the world lie in their hands. And they intend that these decisions shall leave the peoples of each nation free from foreign domination, free for economic, social, and spiritual growth.

Economic freedom is as important as political freedom. Not only must people have access to what other peoples produce, but their own products must in turn have some chance of reaching men all over the world. There will be no peace, there will be no real development, there will be no economic stability, unless we find the method by which we can begin to break down the unnecessary trade barriers hampering the flow of goods. Obviously, the sudden and uncompromising abolition of tariffs after the war could only result in disaster. But obviously, also, one of the freedoms we are fighting for is freedom to trade. I know there are many men, particularly in America, where our standard of living exceeds the standard of living in the rest of the world, who are genuinely alarmed at such a prospect, who believe that any such process will only lessen our own standard of living. The reverse of this is true.

Many reasons may be assigned for the amazing economic development of the United States. The abundance of our national resources, the freedom of our political institutions, and the character of our population have all undoubtedly contributed. But in my judgment the greatest factor has been the fact that by the happenstance of good fortune there was created here in America the largest area in the world in which there were no barriers to the exchange of goods and ideas.

And I should like to point out to those who are fearful one inescapable fact. In view of the astronomical figures our national debt will assume by the end of this war, and in a world reduced in size by industrial and transportation developments, even our present standard of living in America cannot be maintained unless the exchange of goods flows more freely over the whole world. It is also inescapably true that to raise the standard of living of any man anywhere in the world is to raise the standard of living by some slight degree of every man everywhere in the world.

Finally, when I say that this world demands the full par-

ticipation of a self-confident America, I am only passing on
an invitation which the peoples of the East have given us.
They would like the United States and the other United
Nations to be partners with them in this grand adventure.
They want us to join them in creating a new society of independent nations, free alike of the economic injustices of the
West and the political malpractices of the East. But as partners in that great new combination they want us neither
hesitant, incompetent, nor afraid. They want partners who
will not hesitate to speak out for the correction of injustice
anywhere in the world.

Our allies in the East know that we intend to pour out
our resources in this war. But they expect us now—not after
the war—to use the enormous power of our giving to pro-
mote liberty and justice. Other peoples, not yet fighting,
are waiting no less eagerly for us to accept the most chal-
lenging opportunity of all history—the chance to help create a new society in which men and women the world around
can live and grow invigorated by independence and freedom.